FRONTIERS OF JUSTICE
Volume 3: The Crime Zone

Edited by Claudia Whitman & Julie Zimmerman

BIDDLE PUBLISHING COMPANY
PMB 103, PO Box 1305, Brunswick, Maine 04011

PUBLISHER'S CATALOGING IN PUBLICATION DATA

1. Frontiers of Justice, Vol. 3: The Crime Zone
2. Whitman, Claudia, Ed.
3. Zimmerman, Julie, Ed.
4. Criminal Justice
5. United States, Criminal Justice
6. Corrections
7. United States, Corrections
8. Prisons & Prisoners
9. Crime Prevention

Library of Congress Catalog Card No: 00 90028
ISBN 1-879418-30-4

Published in the United States of America by
        Biddle Publishing Company
        PMB 103, PO Box 1305
        Brunswick, Maine 04011
        207-833-5016

Art work by Matthew Matteo. All rights reserved.

"The frontier is the outer edge of the wave -- the meeting point between savagery and civilization...the line of most rapid and effective Americanization."

Frederick Jackson Turner, 1894
<u>The Significance of the Frontier in American History</u>

This book is dedicated to:
A.J. Bannister
Clifford Boggess
Brian Baldwin
Billy Hughes

TABLE OF CONTENTS

INTRODUCTION
Steve J. Martin

I am deeply honored to have this opportunity to contribute the Introduction to this most worthy and inspiring volume, for it has caused me to reflect on a near three decades of work with both the keepers and the kept. I was drawn to my career as a corrections professional by two major influences. The first was my mother, a career caregiver, who always looked for the good in those with whom she came in contact through almost 50 years as a registered nurse. She closed her career by helping to establish a hospice for the terminally ill in her hometown community. The second, the teachings of Christ, most especially the Beatitudes, which in some fashion, regardless of religious preference, surely must guide or influence most caregivers.

When I entered the profession some 30 years ago, the rehabilitation model was the accepted paradigm for corrections professionals. This was a model through which caregivers could flourish. This model has long since been abandoned for the punishment model through which caretakers flourish. Caregivers are hopeful and generally have a core belief in the dignity and worth of those to whom they administer. Their efforts are therefore geared toward facilitating positive growth, an exercise steeped in hope and optimism. The caretaker accepts his charges as he finds them and directs his efforts toward devising more enterprising and efficient ways in which to maintain them until his caretaking responsibilities end.

This caretaking mentality has given us "supermax prisons" in a "no frills" environment where we keep that dreaded demon, the "super predator." It has provided the basis for which America, with under 5% of the world's population, will have 25% of the world's prison inmates. It has given us the "corrections industrial complex" in which confined persons are reduced to commodities to be brokered by those who embrace the profit motive to the exclusion of basic principles of sound correctional management. It has provided the political framework in which we blithely execute mentally retarded and juvenile offenders. It has provided a basis for Congress to pass a law that prohibits a prisoner from even bringing a federal civil action for mental or emotional suffering without a prior showing of physical injury. It has provided a basis for a federal appeals court to hold officials blameless for allowing an inmate to die from bedsores.

It is no small irony that in this age of punitive zealotry and conservatism, those who are the subject of these fatalistic contemporary philosophies are the ones who write most eloquently and optimistically about

7

them. It is a dangerous proposition to dismiss their writings as the utterances of failed persons who have nothing to contribute to a civilized society. It is the height of arrogance and folly to ignore any person, regardless of prior bad acts, who is attempting to articulate a message of hope and redemption. In a fashion, such persons are the real experts on the efficacy of our criminal justice policies. For those who embrace this attitude, they open themselves to a wonderful learning experience by reading such a volume as <u>Frontiers of Justice</u>.

I will close this Introduction with the eloquent words of a convict:

I know not whether Laws be right,
or whether Laws be wrong;
all that we know who lie in gaol
is that the wall is strong;
and that each day is like a year,
a year whose days are long.

But this I know, that every Law
that men have made for Man,
since first Man took his brother's life,
and the sad world began,
but straws the wheat and saves the chaff
with a most evil fan.

This too I know -- and wise it were
if each could know the same --
that every prison that men build
is built with bricks of shame,
and bound with bars lest Christ should see
how men their brothers maim.

With bars they blur the gracious moon,
and blind the goodly sun:
and they do well to hide their Hell,
for in it things are done
that Son of God nor son of Man
ever should look upon!
                    Oscar Wilde, from "The Ballad of Reading Gaol," 1898

Steve J. Martin is in private practice as a corrections consultant and is actively involved in prison litigation in such states as California, New York, Ohio, Maryland, Montana and Utah. He is involved in jail litigation in such cities as New York City, Pittsburgh and Milwaukee. He is serving as expert to the U.S. Department of Justice, Civil Rights Division, in both prison and jail cases in South Carolina, Mississippi and Nevada. He has worked as a consultant in more than 20 states and has visited or inspected more than 500 confinement facilities in the U.S. He received his B.S. and M.A. in Correctional Administration from Sam Houston State University and his J.D. from the University of Tulsa. During his more than 25 years in the criminal justice field, Steve has worked as a prison guard, probation and parole officer and prosecutor. He is the former General Counsel of the Texas prison system as well as having served gubernatorial appointments in Texas on both a sentencing commission and a council for mentally impaired offenders. Steve coauthored a book on Texas prisons and has written numerous articles on criminal justice issues. He has served as an adjunct faculty member at six different universities, including the University of Texas School of Law. He currently resides in Austin, Texas.

PROLOGUE

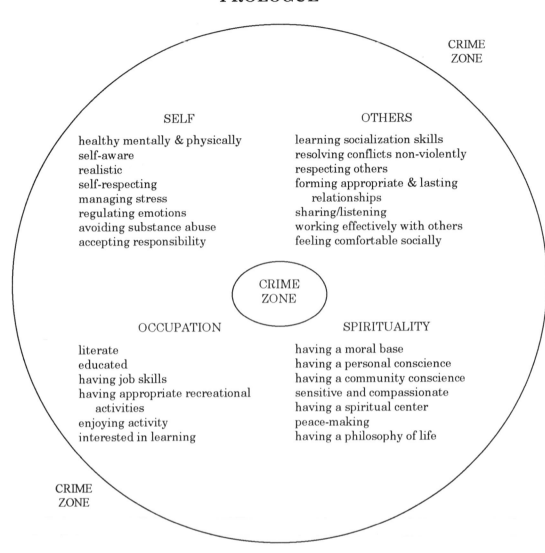

The above model is appropriate for everyone, law abiding citizen or convicted offender. We all juggle the various demands of our life, none of us doing it perfectly. Generally our self-images, relationships with others, moral/spiritual outlook, and ability to work and play exist in some kind of equilibrium, and we can function in life without endangering ourselves or others. A serious problem in any one of these areas, however, can disrupt the overall balance, and, of course, some individuals never have a chance as children to take even the preliminary steps toward a happy, healthy future. For many Americans, the result is a gradual sinking or an explosion into the Crime Zone.

Conversely, an individual can focus and grow in any one area as the first step to coming out of the Crime Zone. That first step can then affect other qualities which build on each other to allow the individual to grow and change. Even prisoners serving life sentences or on death row have found a way out of the Crime Zone. Some of the avenues out include substance abuse programs, spiritual awakening, therapeutic communities, vocational training, educational programs, or an undiscovered talent for the arts. Advancement in any of these gradually promotes self respect and improved relationships with others. This, in turn, begins to bring life into balance. This balance is not an absolute for any of us. It is an ongoing process and it is not solely determined by our environments: **whether in or out of prison, we can be in or out of the Crime Zone.**

The writers, artists and poets of this volume have all been in the Crime Zone. Their contributions represent the painful, difficult task of sharing the experiences, choices and thinking that led to their offenses. We may scorn them for their crimes, but we should also credit them for working to redefine their lives. They are climbing from the lowest place people in our society can fall -- as convicted, violent offenders -- to find self-knowledge, positive direction, sobriety, education, vocational and artistic skills, compassion and faith. We all struggle to reach and maintain these goals; they are reaching them in the often brutal and sterile environment of prison. Like many of us, some continue to have conflicted feelings about their pasts, aware that the journey toward habilitation is not yet complete. Each discovers a unique combination of programs and approaches that feels right and seems to work, all determined to find the best within themselves. And yes, they do live with remorse for the crimes that were committed in earlier years.

We hope this volume will allow the reader to see these prisoners in a new light, as people who have grown and changed and are willing to help us understand the roots of crime and recidivism and the factors that encourage crime prevention and habilitation. These are the experts whose experiences can teach us about the Crime Zone.

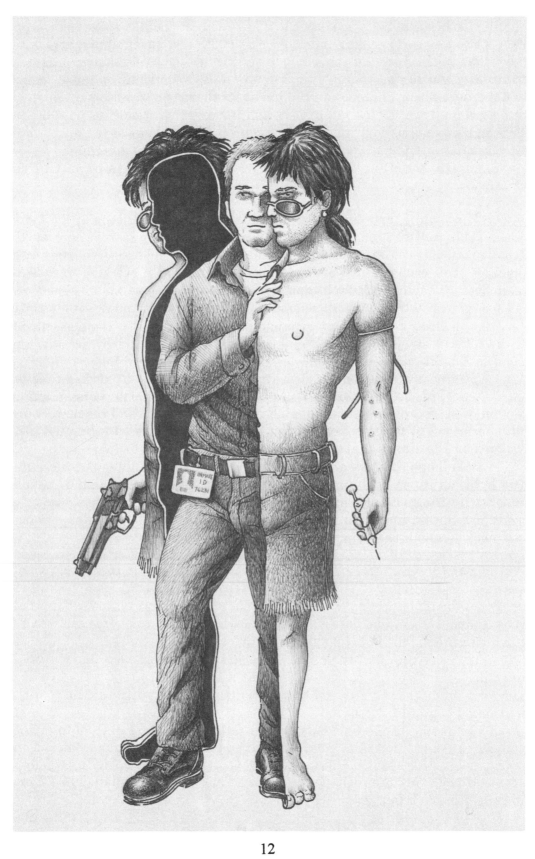

12

THE SEARCH FOR HOME

Russell Scott Day

It would be easy to sit here and complain about what's wrong with this prison system, to pass judgement on those who oversee its functioning. It would also be easy to point out the ridiculous rhetoric of our politicians, the "get tough on crime" jargon that's been preached for over a decade. I could ask you to look at the darker sides of our social order and its insatiable need for vengeance. I could talk about these things because they all play a role in the dysfunction of corrections, but instead I will share my personal insights with you. Having been locked up for the last 14 years, since the age of 15, I will tell you how the Department of Corrections has impacted me.

I grew up in a home that had lost its sense of family values. My mother has been an alcoholic for over 20 years. Our family was poor, and the people around us either drank or used drugs in some form or another. There was minimal parental supervision. I was a boy with the freedom to roam as I desired.

And I roamed a lot. It was easier than facing the pain at home, pain that instilled in me feelings of worthlessness, guilt and resentment. A child roaming the streets is susceptible to many things and I was exposed to most of them. I became addicted to drugs, quick elixirs to escape the chaotic realities surrounding me. I became victim to a multitude of physical and sexual abuses. Crime became a convenient resource, not only to support my addictions, but to gain my mother's attention. Negative attention was better than none at all. These became the patterns of my life, the things that would lead me into the lonely confines of a cell. I wasn't mature enough to understand what would come about from my actions. I didn't know there were other choices. I'm not making excuses; I'm simply pointing out the way my life evolved.

My drug use, and the crime spree it sparked eventually landed me in Juvenile Detention at the age of 15. That was in 1985. From what I've seen and read in the local news, the place has changed very little in 14 years. If anything, it's gotten worse.

I walked into the unit I was assigned to on that first day; 30 to 40 kids were spread out at tables in a dayroom, all of them quiet as church mice, doing paperwork. It was spooky, almost surreal. At the far end two adults sat behind a table, overlooking the room. I had no idea what was taking place, but I'd soon find out. And I'd rebel.

13

Juvenile Detention believes every kid that comes through its doors has the potential to be a career criminal. They believe it's their job to break down these patterns of thinking before they take hold. They use dominance, authority, manipulation and fear tactics to do this. Their rules and programs are formatted to address the criminal, not the child who resorted to crime. I'd received negative reinforcement all my life. When I rebelled against a system telling me I was something I wasn't, I gained the negative reinforcement I was accustomed to. I learned to be a criminal in Juvenile Detention.

Staff in Juvenile Detention rarely spoke to kids on a humane level. They presided over us, speaking only to order us into action or to correct us on an infraction of the rules. I felt like a dog being taught new tricks, the staff the ones pulling my leash.

Once I was caught talking about running away. Two male staff members pulled me into an isolated dorm. The first got in my face, screaming, spittle flying from his lips: "You think you're something special? You're just a punk! I know! I grew up with punks like you in Boston! You'll be somebody's bitch in prison! You don't believe me? You calling me a liar?" I was grinning at him. His threats didn't scare me -- I'd been through worse. The other staff member, though, made me think. "Is this how you want the rest of your life to be?"

"No," I answered.

"Then why do you keep doing this?" It was a question I had no answer for at the time.

There were staff who spoke with us in counseling sessions, teachers who encouraged us to learn and grow. I'd been put on a program where I wore shackles all day because I'd escaped so many times. My teacher, Mr. McDevitt, took a special interest in me, taking the time to learn my interests so he could incorporate them into my learning. He also walked me to the library every day, my only time outdoors, and we'd just talk about life in general. He treated me like a person. Unfortunately, these people are few and their efforts are swamped by the majority, strict authoritarians demanding complete control. Though grateful to the few, I frequently broke rules to maintain my own sense of control and humanity.

Here are a couple of examples I can recall on how kids are handled at the Youth Center, outdated approaches to rehabilitation by insufficiently trained staff who think of children as career criminals. It felt like our childhoods were stripped away and ignored.

I was confined in a segregation cell, battling fits of depression at the time. They were talking about giving custody of me to the State as neither of my parents was willing to take me back. I felt abandoned and unloved and was blaming myself for all of my problems. I was such a horrible person, I didn't deserve to be anyone's son; I was such a horrible person, I didn't deserve to be a part of any family. As time passed, my feelings of guilt, isolation and loneliness grew. I began to wonder if I deserved to live at all, wishing I'd never been born to begin with.

I began to consider suicide daily, thinking of ways I could end my life. I didn't want to die, but I couldn't see any other way to escape the turmoil I felt inside. I was also scared. I didn't want to suffer a painful and unpleasant death, and I still had the desperate hope for a brighter tomorrow.

I started playing a very dangerous game -- I plotted staged hangings in my cell. I'd watch the staff circle the cells to do count. I'd have myself and my noose ready; as they'd peer into my window, I'd drop. A couple times I came close, dropping too soon or when a nervous guard fumbled to get his keys. If any one thing had gone wrong, I wouldn't be alive today. Part of me wanted to die, while that other part was crying out in the only way it knew how.

After a few attempts, the staff took it seriously enough to send me to the shrink. Dr. S. was a tall man with strange, wide eyes and a phony smile of sparkling razor blades. He looked, for lack of a better term, psychotic.

"I understand you want to kill yourself," he said, offering his fiendish grin.

"I've thought about it," I said.

"I've been told you tried to hang yourself," he added.

"If that's what they say," I replied.

"That's the worst way to kill yourself," he said. "There's really no guarantee you'll succeed. Besides, it takes too long. First, your body starts convulsing uncontrollably. If you survive, you'll probably be a vegetable, able to think, but unable to move or talk. If you don't, well, it's messy. Your body loses all its functions. You piss and shit in your pants as you die."

He was telling me horror stories I'd already heard. He was trying to scare me and make me think, but he was also playing with me. He didn't think I was serious about committing suicide. "If I was going to kill myself," he continued, "I'd put a shotgun in my mouth and pull the trigger. Better yet, just under the chin. That way there's less chance the bullet will ricochet off the skull. It's a little messy, blowing your brains all over the place, but it's a guaranteed way to die."

He fell silent, looking at me with that phony, shark-like smile. I looked him straight in the eyes and said four words: "You got a gun?" He didn't take kindly to that, but I didn't care. He was pre-judging me like so many others, without knowing who I was or why I felt the way I did. Anyone who even thinks of suicide has problems that need to be discussed and resolved. The great moral structure of this institution didn't see it that way. It only saw a con playing a game to get attention.

The Youth Center is based on a level system. The better your level, the more privileges you get. Level one is the best, four the worst; how well you follow the rules determines your level status. At the time of another incident, I was on level one. I was looking forward to going home for a weekend leave. Waiting in anticipation, wanting to be with my family and away from the strict rules of the institution, I tried to keep my mind occupied so I wouldn't get over-excited as the time for my leave approached.

While waiting, I was working on math homework, sitting quietly at a desk trying to solve the problems in front of me. I was completely engrossed in what I was doing. The Unit Director, or head staff member, came up and asked me a question. I was so caught up in what I was doing, I didn't hear her. "Huh?" I responded, hoping she'd repeat the question.

"'Huh?' Did you say 'huh' to me? You don't say 'huh' to me. You say, 'Yes, Missus.' That's it. That's a level three write-up for disrespect to staff." (Disrespect to staff, one of many generalized code violations that every institution has.) The write-up meant that I'd lost my level one status. I was now level three, meaning I'd just lost my weekend leave. I couldn't believe it. I hadn't done anything wrong. If anything, I was being productive by doing my homework. In essence, I'd only asked what she had said. My shock slowly changed to anger. I was being unfairly stripped of my leave after working so hard for it. I wanted to lash out at an unjust system, but I bit my lip. I wrote a letter instead and argued my position.

I was given my leave, though it was made to sound like I had been given a gift instead of having earned it. I later learned this had been a test to see if I could handle the pressures of a weekend leave. They wanted to see if I'd snap. I wouldn't give them the satisfaction; I waited until after my leave to go off.

Unfortunately, this is the way many institutions operate. They give you hope, telling you to work hard to gain certain rewards. Then, on the threshold of success, they pull the carpet out from under you and tell you to start all over again. Hope is the greatest treasure for a desperate soul behind institutional walls. It's also the most fragile.

The staff didn't show compassion or a true desire to understand. Corrections Officers were there to condemn us for every petty rule broken, rules they created to establish order and discipline, not morality and virtue. Over time, you learn how to manipulate this system. You learn to think like a criminal, the very thing they're supposed to be stopping. Children don't commit crimes because they're criminals. There's something missing in their lives; poverty, drug addiction, low self-esteem, peer pressure and various forms of abuse can all lead to crime. Perhaps a child is isolated from his peers or lacks emotional support at home. There's usually a lot taking place behind the negative behavior. Until we recognize and treat juvenile offenders as children, they'll continue to evolve into criminals.

It's difficult at times to reflect and contemplate what may have changed my own life as a boy. I grew up with two parents who concealed all their emotions, except anger. I learned that my emotions were my problem, not things to trouble everyone else with. I became a recluse, not trusting my peers or adults. All I'd ever received from either was grief.

For my life to change as a boy, I believe it would've taken a cooperative community effort on many levels. At least one of my parents would have needed to face the harsh realities of their own dysfunction. School counselors would have needed to act as mediators between myself and peer groups to help in a slow process of bringing both sides together through calm but open communication. Most of all, I needed a long term role model to believe in and encourage me. The wounds of low self-esteem were being infected daily with new ridicule and phrases of negative opinion. This would have been a slow process, demanding patience, tolerance and encouragement through positive reinforcement. I sincerely believe that such a commitment is the only way my life would have evolved differently.

I don't believe children want to be criminals. Crime is a symptom of other problems and it's my firm belief that more is achieved by gentle approaches than through disciplinary settings. After Juvenile Detention, the Department of Corrections placed me in a new setting to learn about my diabetes. It was a live-in hospital with school, counseling and recreational facilities. I was given a very warm and friendly welcome. It was awkward and my hello's were bashfully quiet. I'd never experienced such open kindness before. Not once was I told what to do. Instead, different programs were recommended, but the ultimate choice was mine. One program, teaching assertive rather than aggressive interaction, I initially didn't want to do. "Just give it a try," one of the counselors said. "I think you'll find it useful. If you don't, we can try something else." I learned a great deal from that class.

Staff were always personally involved, taking into account our interests and concerns. They took us on hikes, played games with us, let us listen to music we chose and talked with us personally. They were caring people with a real interest. I excelled through the programs, becoming a role model for other kids and learning valuable skills along the way. I was happier there than I'd ever been in my life. It only lasted three months. It was too short a term, but it did work. For that time, and even in parts of myself today, it had changed me. If only it could have lasted longer.

Without moral guidance, no understanding of responsibility and with many of the issues in my life still unresolved, I was released at the age of 18 to re-enter society. Mentally and emotionally I hadn't matured at all. I was still very much a child, but legally recognized as an adult. With no encouragement or support system to rely on, I soon reverted back to drugs to escape the pains and pressures of life. I still didn't know any other way. Drug use again led to crime and eventually into the degrading field of prostitution. This isn't the life I wanted, but it's all I knew, all I saw. All of this only reinforced that I was worthless, that I was scum and that my life would never add up to anything. It was a time of depression and loneliness, of not caring if I lived or died. I contemplated suicide daily and attempted it on half a dozen occasions. I couldn't even die right. I didn't care about anything anymore, my life or anyone else's. I resigned myself to being one of the world's great failures and I wandered aimlessly through the days, trying desperately to stay one step ahead of the misery.

But the misery won out. It tracked me down and washed over me like a violent tidal wave. In one brief moment, all the pain and tragedy of my life burst out in the ultimate act of senseless rebellion. I killed a man. I stabbed him to death.

That happened on January 26, 1990. The years since have been a long, arduous journey, one I've often had to travel alone. When people see me, they

17

see only a murderer, not the person I am or the circumstances that led to this tragic event. They see a cold-blooded killer, not the boy who fought to become a man, searching for understanding and ways to redeem his own humanity. My biggest support on this journey are the most loathsome of people, the convicts who surround me, who offer what advice and wisdom they have to share. Sometimes a step toward maturity came with other convicts telling me to wake up, often with words not so kind!

I've come to understand that my life has been a constant attempt to escape the pains I felt and, by doing so, I've visited that pain onto loved ones and strangers alike. That hasn't sat well with me. I've come to realize the truth that life is what we make of it and today I strive to make mine a good one. Many torments and struggles have gone into these realizations. Hours of personal reflection and the support of murderers, thugs and thieves have allowed me to mature into the person I've always wanted to be. Guilt over the man I'd killed and grief over what I'd put my family through were heavy burdens. The process would be a long and painful one.

To reach my goal of a decent life, I had to achieve two fundamental things: I had to find success where I'd found only failure before, and I had to come to terms with my past.

I began by taking college classes. Education is important, not only for one's future, but for empowering one with knowledge as well. High school had been a nightmare for me, but college was on my terms. Through introductory courses in Psychology and Sociology, I learned a lot about myself. English 101, run by Henry Saunders, re-ignited a love I have for creative writing. This love was later enhanced, thanks to a professor from one of the State colleges, Jaimee Colbert, who for six years came in once a month to do a creative writing workshop. Not only did my ability to write mature, but so did my friendship with her and with the other writers involved.

I participated in sports functions, improving year by year until I'd achieved a new level of self confidence. I worked hard within the prison's Industrial Shop for two years. This was a big success for me as I'd had 17 different jobs when I was a free man. Holding a job for two years may seem insignificant to some, but it was a stepping stone for me, a building block that helped to affirm my value and worth as a person. I became involved in non-profit groups like the National Junior Chamber of Commerce and the NAACP. They were social programs at work for people and communities. I helped to make a difference in peoples' lives. I underwent substance abuse counseling and participated in a program of meditation, all to enhance an understanding of and balance within myself. Most importantly, I became deeply involved in religious functions. This has become the foundation upon which everything else stands.

There is no doubt in my mind that spirituality was the core for helping me turn my life around, even though the spiritual path I chose is not conventional by the larger society's standards. In hindsight, I've studied many spiritual roads and the one thing I've learned is that they all offer the same basic things. They offer a direction, a way in which one can view his life and the world he exists in. All of them contain a value system, a positive moral framework to work from and build one's character by. In prison, where everything has an aura of negativity and perversion looming overhead, a spiritual path is sometimes the only way to keep a positive outlook on life. It's the key place where I find the strength to hope and the resilient courage to dream.

I think the same is true for many people in here. Let's face it, most guys are in jail for doing pretty bad things; it's obvious something was out of whack with their values on the streets. Prison is a reflection of the messed up world they've known. I've met many men who were given a brief glimpse of a different life through spirituality. Most of these men were encouraged by these brief glimpses and dared to contemplate a new and better life. Many even had the guts to pursue the dream, as I did, and their lives were forever changed.

Here in the Maine State Prison, the administration has been very open to such pursuits over recent years. There are both Catholic and Protestant services, a Muslim gathering, a Native American group, a Wiccan coven and, most recently, an Asatru Kindred. There is something for just about every type of individual to embrace. There is even a meditation program as part of the substance abuse department. The only difficulties, sadly, come from one prison chaplain who seems to have little tolerance for faiths not Christian. His personal feelings have caused problems on occasion for those trying to follow their own callings, but the commitment and persistence of these inmates, as well as a prison administration tolerant of positive religious expression, have counter-balanced these difficulties.

I find the prejudice of any one faction personally sad. We need all paths and as much positive enlightenment for our prisoners as we can find. I've always believed that religion is important to a full and balanced existence. It promotes positive direction and moral teachings that embrace a reverence and love for life. When our prisoners, our outcasts, pursue such directions, we as loving people need to support and encourage those efforts. Not all of us may agree with a particular religious belief, but I believe we can agree that religion gives those who pursue it a positive direction in their lives. It can only help to enrich our society as a whole and help to bring out the humanity in all of us.

Prejudice, on the other hand, perverts the very spirit of our humanity and prejudice runs rampant in prison -- from racial gangs, to the separation between convicts and cops, and the difference in the way we as a culture look at the felon as opposed to the non-felon. All institutional dynamics are vulnerable to prejudice over fairness.

Every prison, for example, has its rules. They're meant to maintain security and keep inmates and staff safe. Too often they become convenient tools to punish, torment and harass people. One such rule is that no inmate can swap and/or receive anything from another inmate. This rule exists to circumvent gambling debts and strong arm tactics to intimidate one out of his personal property. This in itself is a good thing, but officers feeling irritated or vindictive can, and have, used this rule as a way to get even for something as minor as sharing a cigarette or a cup of coffee. In other words, we can actually be punished for being generous, by extending a courtesy to a friend that everyone on the outside would accept as normal. Most importantly, at the end of every rule book, a copy of which every inmate gets upon arriving here, are nine words that make the rest of the booklet useless: "All these rules are subject to change without notice." Additionally, all the rules are worded with generalities, allowing for broad interpretation. This allows guards to hold the future of every inmate in their hands and this is a power often misused.

Here's a recent event to consider. There's a section of the prison for prisoners who aren't considered problems. They're afforded privileges other inmates don't have. One such privilege is a chance to take a shower in the early evening. Each inmate at this time is, by rule, given ten minutes to bathe. This rule is rarely enforced and the inmates generally police themselves to give everyone a chance to clean up. Recently, one inmate was singled out and harassed for taking 15 minutes. There was no security risk or lives in jeopardy. Because the guard had problems with this inmate, the rule was utilized as a weapon to degrade and harass this individual. This man didn't commit a crime -- he was in the shower five extra minutes, that's all. What has he learned? That he's a pawn in a sick power play. He's learned his value as a human being isn't worth a 15 minute shower.

These things happen every day, to greater and lesser degrees. Anyone forced to live under such conditions would become angry. The problem is, we're putting criminals in this environment, people we want to change. Instead, too often they leave a little angrier, a little more rebellious. They commit more crimes, worse crimes, and they return to a system that only encourages this trend. Prisons are full of negative crap and it's easy to get weighed down and discouraged. It takes a determined person not to fall victim to the harassment and insults of guards and inmates alike.

Even in such hostile surroundings, there are single rays of light peeking through. It could be a guard who thanks you every time you finish your job, a counselor or religious volunteer taking a personal interest in your life. It could be an inmate who's been through your struggle and shares what he's learned, or maybe a nurse who says, "Good morning." These are small and insignificant in themselves, but in a place full of animosity, corruption and anger, they're the sparks that keep the hopeful man hoping. You've got to hold onto such things with a death grip in prison, because if you lose these few rays of sun, your soul dies here. So you hold on and hope the sun shines tomorrow too.

Most people commit a crime out of a feeling of necessity. I thought I needed to escape my pains. Perhaps somebody else needed to pay the bills. For some reason, their ability to cope was flawed. Yes, prisons must be secure, but not to the point where we're losing the human quality of the person we're locking up. Over 90% of the people in jail today will be released. Do we really want to take away what positive qualities or humanity they might still have left? We need things to encourage growth of one's humanity, support structures for the attempts that are made. We've mastered the art of locking these doors, but continue to fail when it comes to encouragement and incentives. We can recognize that both are needed for the good of our society.

I came to prison with a 30 year sentence. I was 20 years old. I knew I was getting out one day and that I had to start getting my life together right away. I had to gain self-esteem, self-responsibility and find a new way to view the tragic world I grew up in. I was able to set aside the anger I'd felt, to cope with the pain that had created that anger. Nobody has acknowledged this, though they should. People believe I'm a worthless murderer, that I'm a useless convict not worthy of affection or freedom. They judge my character on the failures of my past instead of celebrating the transitions that have been made. Once I begin to believe the rhetoric, my life is done. So I fight on, rebelliously, wanting to prove everyone wrong.

I fear the future. In roughly nine years I'll be a free man. I've seen so many injustices here. I wonder what resentments I'll carry with me. My family's still poor; they can do little more than encourage me. I don't have a career. Being locked up at the age of 15, I've never had the chance to learn one. Besides, who will want to hire a man whose spent two decades behind bars? Where will I live? Will my neighbors want to talk to me? Who will I talk to when the burden of freedom becomes too much? Who will understand? I really want to work with troubled kids, reach them before they reach these tragic halls. I want to get married and raise a family, to do charity work in my spare time.

The future's so uncertain, so scary. Will I be a murderer or a man with the chance to try and make up for a single moment in time that went dreadfully wrong? I wonder if there is a place for me beyond these walls. Only time will tell. I don't know, but I hope so. I sure as hell hope so. What's this struggle for if there's no place to call home at the end of the road?

Russell Scott Day is a Maine native who has been writing for over 15 years. His poetry has been published in <u>Trapped Under Ice: A Death Row Anthology</u>, <u>The Cafe Review</u> and <u>Coastlines</u>. His fiction has appeared in <u>Flying Horse</u> and "Rogue's Gallery." Russell is incarcerated at the Maine State Prison where he is the Secretary of the Long Timer's Group, Secretary of the National Junior Chamber of Commerce, a Board Member of the Pagan Wiccan Group and Spirtuality Editor of the Internet magazine <u>CellDoor</u>. He has worked with children through mail correspondence and took part in the documentary "Choices," (produced by the Rockport Film School and Maine D.O.C.), a video of prisoners reaching out to troubled youth. Russell is presently working on his autobiography and a collection of poetry. His favorite quote: "Life's a journey, not a destination." (Aerosmith)

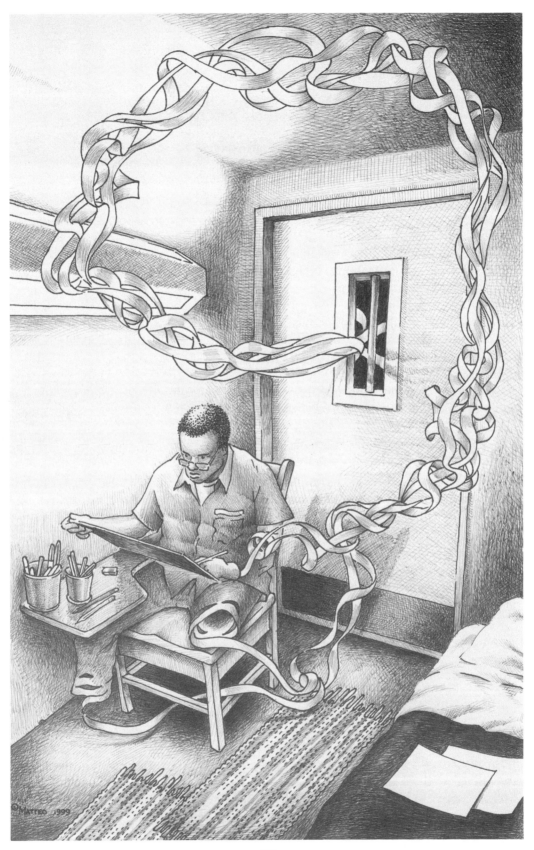

23

THROUGH THE NARROW GATE

Calbraith MacLeod

I'm a machinist by trade. I live in one of a range of prison cells housing the former owner of an industrial supply business, a truck driver, an apartment manager, a baker, a building contractor, a coordinator of a day center for the developmentally disabled, a scientist who's worked for NASA, a window glazer, an auto-body technician, a radio disc jockey, a professional piano tuner, a house painter and a cabinet builder. Four of my neighbors have general education diplomas, five graduated high school and four hold college degrees. Seven of my neighbors are veterans. We've all been married. We all have children who love and miss us, and all but two of us owned homes. All of us owned cars when we were free -- cars that were registered, inspected and insured. We didn't steal them.

On the street, we'd awakened in the mornings, disliked the idea of getting out of bed, but had arisen nonetheless. We'd driven to our jobs, sworn at the traffic and stopped to buy a pack of cigarettes or a cup of coffee along the way. We'd all worried over making our house and car payments and wondered how we were going to pay the electric, phone, heat and credit card bills. Some of us had drunk too much alcohol, acted belligerent and felt bad about it afterwards. Some of us hadn't drunk alcohol at all.

Today, in America, we daily face the hatred of thousands of people towards us. Perhaps no group of people since the American Indian has been assaulted by such a concerted effort of hatred. Everywhere newspaper writers, television reporters, former coworkers, former neighbors, politicians we'd supported, police our taxes had paid the wages of, professionals we'd respected, prison employees and occasionally our own family members refer to us as scum, losers, predators and animals. As convicted people, we are caged, beaten and, on occasion, systematically killed by our fellow human-beings.

Year upon year of disparagement and ostracism, year upon year of being caged, randomly stripped naked, our belongings arbitrarily searched or taken pressures us to believe ourselves to be no more than animals. As the years pass, it becomes harder and harder to remember what we are. There are more than a few unfortunate souls who have forgotten. They become so indiscriminately violent they need be isolated from the rest of the prison population; or they become so distanced from reality they squat, dirty and disheveled, in the corners of our prisons, talking to imaginary listeners and smoking cigarette butts they've rescued from the ground.

As convicted people, it is important we remember we came from a social world so we have some chance of returning to live in it, relate to it and leave it with the dignity of human-beings. No matter what the media, our captors or their agents refer to us as, it is important that we do not think of ourselves as scum, predators and animals. It is important we do not adopt the idea -- they treat me like an animal so I will act like one. For the moment we give in to either of these temptations, we dramatically reduce the chance we will be able to get back on track toward the wholesome visions we all once harbored about how our lives as human beings are supposed to unfold.

None of us wanted to be criminals. We did not sit in our fifth grade social studies classes and dream of spending our lives in conflict with the law. We dreamed of having homes and jobs and grown up toys. We dreamed of leading serene, sane, non-destructive lives. Although many people, both in and out of prison, do not want convicts to be at peace in prison, it is our early dreams of serenity we as prisoners need to re-discover if we are to transform our lives into demonstrations worthy of self-respect. Further, it is only in developing a feeling of inner peace that we who will be released from prison can hope to live in society for long as non-destructive citizens. In fact, regardless of our optimistic fantasies of being able to control ourselves "this time" when we get out, if we do not develop a sense of serenity in prison, there exists small chance our behavior as free people will be any different than before we were imprisoned. The inability to create a feeling of serenity while living with society is what initially sparked many a convicted person's criminal exploits.

Fortunately, even when we've fallen far from the mark and face the hatred of a billion people, as long as we remember we're humans, we maintain the capacity for self-respect. I believe the fact that we each own the ability to lead ourselves to a place of serenity while under any adversity is the most awesome power we as humans possess. I hope, by the end of this chapter, you will understand how that can occur.

I am the third child of six born to married parents. My childhood occurred during the late 50's and throughout the 60's. My family owned a home and a little land, but not much else. My father was a WWII veteran, as patriotic as a man can be. But I don't think the war did him any favors. I've seen him leap, startled as a rabbit, at the sound of fireworks on the 4th of July. I've also seen him stand by with punctured lungs after an auto accident and refuse medical treatment until the doctor had examined his son's injuries. I've also watched him rape my mother. He ordered me to watch. It was a game: he'd rape her, he said, because she beat me. I'd watch as the humiliation part of her punishment, then she'd beat me when my father was at work.

I don't think my mother was ever able to love children. She held me in a loving manner twice in my life. Maybe she just didn't know how to be loving. Her own mother died when she was young, so maybe that had something to do with it. I know she hated me. I can't really blame her given the recurring circumstances. Still, I hated her for not showing me the affection I deserved and I hated her for beating me. She once threw me with such fury, my head struck a bureau hard enough to knock me unconscious. I can imagine my father lifting my limp body from the floor, screaming at my mother for having killed me. But of course I didn't die.

My father died of tuberculosis when I was twelve. For the next two years, my mother beat me every night upon her return from her second shift job, except one night when my sister hid my father's leather belt, my mom's weapon of choice. After a year or so, I got so used to "the belt," it just didn't hurt anymore; I couldn't even cry. It was as though my tears were all used up. The only problem was that when I didn't cry, my mother became so furious and out of breath from swinging the belt, I was afraid she would give herself a heart attack. So I started to fake crying. After I turned 14, my mother struck me with the buckle end of the belt one night. She'd never done that before; there had always been an unspoken rule against it. That night I took the belt away from her and told her it was over, she would hit me no more. She went to her room and cried for a couple of hours and never raised a hand to me again.

I entered adulthood with no self-respect, no concrete values and enough hatred to have fueled a world war. I felt like an intruder in a world belonging to other people. I believed something was wrong with me. Other people always seemed happy; they appeared to easily understand how to act, what to do and when to do it. I, however, felt a need to plan how to act from moment to moment. Life presented a continuous struggle to be what I thought others wanted me to be. I felt relaxed only when drunk, high or with people I'd already learned how to please. The people I spent time with were not my friends. I looked a part of the group, but secretly I felt alone. I thought other people controlled my life and hated them for controlling me and myself for not stopping them. My inability to control my life filled me with rage.

I began campaigns to change people to my liking. I threatened people so they'd do what I wanted them to do; I manipulated people so they'd act how I wanted them to act; and I lied to people so they'd believe what I wanted them to believe. My efforts to change others became as much work and delivered as much frustration as had my efforts to change myself from moment to moment to suit others. Every lie I told needed to be remembered and followed up. Every threat needed to be repeated, and every manipulation needed to be updated. I ended up depressed, frustrated and suicidal.

My greatest disappointments were that I'd accomplished nothing. I hadn't changed anyone else, not really. My lies faded and the truth was always waiting to show itself. Memories of my threats and manipulations dwindled and people resumed their old ways of behaving. Even after years of effort, using every method I could find an excuse to employ, I'd not managed to maintain control of one life, not even my own.

Still, I firmly believed in the suggestion that one can do anything if he only tries hard enough. I believed I could solve any problem. When I failed to correct a problem, I believed circumstances, other people or poor luck were at fault. My all-powerful self concept, I assured myself, was not defective. I could, I believed, control my drug and alcohol use; I could control my destructive conduct; I could be content, if only other people acted as I directed, if only I possessed more money, if only I owned the fastest car in my town, if only some "condition" changed.

I married a beautiful woman. I bought a wonderful country home. I fathered lovely children. I built the quickest car in my town. I acquired credit galore and money to waste, and I consumed more alcohol than ever before. I smoked marijuana, took speed, snorted cocaine and ate acid. I lied without guilt or reason, stole anything I could and took pride in my thievery. Fear of one thing or another became my constant companion. My prospects of solving any problem grew remote. I lost any clear identity, ideals or self-respect. My conduct wavered from aggressive to assaultive as I worked to frighten, humiliate and control the world around me. I immersed myself in orgies of sex and drugs and perversity. My beautiful wife became an object of utility to me. I neglected my lovely children. I abused my creditors and I damaged my wonderful home.

I knew that unless I took action to curb my destructive behaviors, I'd soon lose all I considered essential to my existence. As always, I put my great intellect and my "masterful" will to work on the problem. I made resolutions to drink only two cans of beer a night, to go to sleep early, to end my thievery, to stop lying and to be more considerate of relatives, neighbors and friends. None the less, I continued to drink all the alcohol I pleased; I continued to stay up late and to lie and to steal; I continued to be inconsiderate of others. I made promises to be more thoughtful of my wife's feelings; I promised to spend more time with my children; I promised to promptly pay my creditors; I promised to stop hurting my loved ones. However, I continued to be unthinking and self-centered, undependable and hurtful.

I reasoned that working the night shift would create more time to spend with my family; however, when I worked at night, I slept all day. I thought if I invited other people to live at my home, I'd stop abusing my wife, but I continued to psychologically abuse her. I imagined if I stockpiled fruit juice I'd drink that instead of beer, but I continued to get drunk. I supposed staying away from people who stole would help me quit stealing, but my thievery continued. I believed if I gave my wife the money for creditors, she'd keep it safe, but after a few drinks I'd frighten her enough to return the money to me.

I understood I was destroying my relationships, property, reputation, health and finances. In spite of it all, I continued in my destructive ways.

Finally, my cruel behavior towards my wife erupted into hurtful violence, and I was charged with aggravated assault and sentenced to five years in prison. In prison, I was asked to participate in a newly developed program for sex offenders. I wasn't required to do the program, because I wasn't convicted of a sex crime. Nevertheless, I agreed to do what the program coordinator instructed. I would have done whatever necessary to shorten my time in prison.

The program I attended consisted of three meetings each week -- a unit meeting where inmates voiced their gripes about prison conditions and restrictions; a group meeting where several of us would discuss various aspects of our crimes; and a one-on-one meeting with a student of psychology. After six months of going to these meetings, I was released from prison and placed on parole. I didn't feel any different than when I'd gone into the program, but I told myself -- they are professionals, perhaps they know something I don't. Perhaps, I thought, all will now be well and I can get on with a good life.

The conditions of my release included continuing to see a therapist once every two weeks, to attend one group meeting each week and to meet my parole officer once a month. My sessions with my therapist consisted of discussions of the weather. The therapist really didn't seem to care what we talked about. My group meetings were discussions of how things were going for everyone and, according to the participants, everything was always going well. No one was about to expose any problems for fear of their parole being violated. My meetings with my parole officer occurred as scheduled for the first few months, then three months at a time would pass and I would need to call her to find out if she was interested in seeing me.

My parole officer told me she would not violate my parole for drinking or for losing my job, but she would violate my parole if both these things occurred. Since I had been released in a strange town and since, according to her assessment, I was "not an alcoholic," my parole officer agreed with me that bars were a good place for me to meet people. So I went to a different bar every night. I must have wanted to meet a lot of people!

The sad part is that even if my parole officer had not allowed me to drink, I would have. Even if my parole officer had been attentive, I would have abused my wife. Even if the group meeting had been a place I could have told the truth, and even if my therapist had been caring, I would have still participated in destructive conduct. The prison program I had attended was not designed to heal my broken persona. It had done nothing to reduce my fears, self-pity, selfishness or hatred towards myself, others and the world.

I met my second wife in a bar. We got an apartment within a few months. I wanted to love her and provide a decent life for us both, but mixed in with my wish to be a good husband to her were reoccurring desires to dominate and humiliate her. She was strong willed, and I seriously injured her twice during my attempts to force her to do my bidding.

My wife had stayed with me because I had manipulated her into being so dependent upon me she had nowhere to turn. Fortunately, I was placed in prison for leaving the scene of an accident. My incarceration granted her the freedom to become somewhat independent and, courageously, to tell the police of my mistreatment of her. I was sentenced to serve 20 to 40 years in prison for abusing her and causing her injury.

I returned to prison consumed by more hatred than ever towards myself and towards the entire world. I'd felt like I could have blown the entire planet out of space if I'd had the ability. I hated myself, I hated others, I hated animals, I hated flowers or anything of beauty. The Vermont State prison administration was so frightened by me, they contracted a place for me in a Federal penitentiary.

I'd like to report there was something short of pre-testing parents that could have intervened in my childhood. I would like to report that there was something someone could have done to keep me or someone like me from developing into someone who would rob, lie, assault people and injure his wife. However, no one could have changed my mom's past. No one could have changed whatever reason she had become unable to show love or concern for me. No one could have changed whatever reason nothing I did was good enough to please her. Her past was just that, in the past. Her life, our life, appeared normal enough. No one would have had reason to intervene. I do not know what the reason is some women develop the propensity to coldly neglect a son's attempts to gain their love, and to insult, threaten, belittle, shame and hurt him. I do believe that as long as women treat their sons in this way, the world will continue to produce men who coldly insult, threaten, belittle, shame and hurt women. This is not to pass blame. People can only give what they have to give. I do not know what events such mothers have suffered. Perhaps it is a circle; men abuse women, women abuse their sons. Perhaps someone could discuss which came first. Even if my mother had understood that how she treated me could have had ramifications for others, could she have overcome the influences of her past and treated me differently?

My wife loved me. I was her world and she worked hard to please me. I rewarded her continuous attempts to conform to my desires with ridicule and more demands, no matter how much she sacrificed her comfort, self-respect and even her individuality, but she actively defended my abusive conduct. She lied to others to protect me. Her loyalty was complete.

I'm describing her loyalty because it is not unlike the loyalty of a son toward an abusive mother. You will find very few convicted people who will speak unkindly of his or her parents. If you suggest the convict was abused, he may turn and hurt you! A man who was abused by his mother will frequently say and even believe it was his father who was at fault. In any event, from listening to many convicts and from my own experience, I believe you will be hard pressed to find many convicted people who were not subjected as children to some type of psychological or mental abuse or deficit of love, hugs and sometimes any warmth or recognition at all. Many convicts were frustrated children; no matter what we did it was not enough to please some significant adult in our lives. A distinct pattern, no matter how hidden, exists, parent to child, child to victim.

I feel fortunate to have been blessed with a good mind. In my efforts to be acceptable, to deserve even a miniscule show of affection, I became, as many convicts do, resourceful and creative. It seemed a necessity. Unfortunately, the self-confidence these attributes delivered also presented a major obstacle to my liberation from a criminal lifestyle. As long as I believed I could solve my own problems by my own methods, I could not progress. The only way I could be liberated from my criminal lifestyle was to begin following someone else's instruction. I needed some completely new thoughts to break into the repetitive cycle I was caught up in.

The event of being open to new thought required, in my case, a collapse of my ego, of my self-confidence, combined with an unflattering view of my current self. As critical and liberating as these enlightening events had been, they'd required as a follow up the availability of methods that would lead me out of the criminal lifestyle.

Unfortunately, I found the Federal and the Vermont prison systems offered only partial answers. The Federal prison offered an alcohol/drug abuse program, but it was strictly a program of information, a critical ingredient in a successful alcohol/drug program, but only one ingredient of many necessary and absent. Vermont corrections offered violent offender and sex offender programs which basically operated in the same ways. One is asked to write "thinking reports" when he encounters situations that did or could lead him to victimize someone. The report consists of describing the situation and listing the thoughts, feelings and behavior patterns one experienced. The object of the exercise is to recognize and change distorted thinking patterns and to become able to identify in advance when one is heading toward victimizing behavior so he can intervene in the process. It is thought that the earlier one can recognize he is heading for trouble, the easier it will be for him to intervene.

While the self-awareness this exercise delivers can be useful as a small part of a rehabilitation whole, it is not a whole unto itself. The problem I experienced with the intervention method of rehabilitation is it did nothing to address the underlying desires and hostilities I was experiencing. Though I was able to keep myself from being violent for a short time, I remained as burdened by a lack of self-respect, by hatred and by compulsions to commit crime as I had ever been. I am one of many who confirm it will not be long before a person full of hostility and burdened by compulsions to commit crimes says to heck with this intervention exercise. It just isn't practical, for one so burdened, to live his life in this way. The intervention approach is like telling an alcoholic who is repeatedly arrested for driving drunk that all he needs to do is recognize when he is drunk and get someone to drive him home. This does nothing to address his underlying problems; how long will it be before he can't find someone to drive him home or just doesn't feel like bothering with the exercise?

With the exception of the Chapman University program I attended at the Lompoc Penitentiary, the correctional programs I have been involved with in Federal prison and in the Vermont state prison system have been, as least for me, incomplete programs without a realistic agenda.

1. The programs utilize embarrassment on a group scale, group viewing or listening to personal thinking reports and tape recordings of fantasies as a tool of therapy.

Problem: Most convicted people are convicts partly because they were humiliated as children. But we are not children anymore; we can now choose, and few of us are willing to subject ourselves to what we once suffered when we had no choice in the matter. Most of us made a silent pact years ago that no one would ever humiliate us again.

2. The programs incorporate strategies aimed at getting the convicted person to know how his victim felt.

Problem: We know how our victims felt. We wanted them to feel that way. We were trying to have them feel like we'd felt all our lives. By telling a convicted person that his victim felt frightened, humiliated, hurt and powerless, the program directors are telling him crime holds great power and that his criminal efforts were a success.

3. The correctional programs I've attended have been billed as something one should do because his or her previous behavior was bad for other people and for society.

Problem: While still ensnared in a destructive lifestyle, a convict's first concern is not other people and society. We care about ourselves. We are for the most part egocentric people and need programs designed to utilize that egocentricity. We need programs billed as good for us.

4. The intervention approach includes the expectation that a convicted person will use the methods because of the threat of a return to prison.

Problem: The threat of prison never stopped us from committing crimes before, and now we are familiar, therefore less frightened, of the concept.

5. As a part of one's intervention in destructive behaviors, one is expected to disclose any risky thoughts, behaviors or feelings to a program counselor on the street.

Problem: We do need someone to disclose such things to on the street if we hope to maintain a crime free life. However, we need someone we can trust not to "flip out" or get frightened by what we tell them, else we will never be able to be honest, and such a counselor will be of no use whatsoever. Every convict knows if he told the state counselors the true thoughts or desires he encounters while living on house arrest, probation or parole, the counselor would quickly have him back inside prison. We need someone outside we can tell anything to, and get constructive feedback.

The therapeutic strategies I have experienced in corrections contain the view that the only important thing is to stop the convicted person from committing more crime, no matter how the convict feels, no matter how he must suffer through life, no matter what kind of destructive medication, continuous supervision or continuous fear it takes to ensure non-destructive behaviors. But this approach only encourages convicts, especially younger ones, to develop unrealistic expectations regarding how they, after treatment, are going to be able to lead normal lives. The discouragement that follows will have them saying, "What's the use?" Implying that fear and supervision will keep one on the right track, irrespective of his personal happiness, is a position that causes heartache, frustration and pain, because it promises something it can't deliver -- long-term non-destructive conduct. It leads the falsely guided to a gradual build-up of anger and resentment, setting themselves and others they care greatly about up for eventual harm. Then, when the harm does come, when the convict re-offends, the program directors declare, "See what happens when you don't follow our recommendations!" To imply that all program participants who re-offend didn't develop the ability to stop committing crimes merely because they hadn't tried hard enough and long enough, and because they didn't have a sufficiently positive attitude is a gross insult. I'm but one of the countless number of typical convicts who have applied themselves to numerous correctional programs with dedication and diligence enough to match any recipient of a doctorate degree. Don't tell us that we didn't try hard enough!

What is particularly infuriating is when a program facilitator moans about how hard he found it to fight a particular character flaw. He neglects to say that the character defect was never really an integral part of his make-up. The person who initially developed into a non-destructive lifestyle simply can't understand the criminal lifestyle. If I had a magic wand, I would put some program directors in the shoes of a typical criminal weighted down with compulsions, unstable emotions and no self-respect. After he's struggled to become able to just stop hating himself for a few minutes each day after years of determined effort and many setbacks, then he might begin to understand what I mean. If I could then wish him into the shoes of the person with an obsession for sex, drugs, money or power so strong that he repeatedly hurts those he most cares for, he would, when feeling suicidal, finally get the full message that how we feel on the inside matters a heck of a lot.

All of us can transform ourselves and develop serenity and self-command enough to lead us to living a non-destructive lifestyle. However, we can never, ever gain control over our lives or truly enter into lasting non-destructive lifestyles solely through the methods of supervision, fear and staged intervention.

It is true that to enter a non-destructive lifestyle, we convicted people need a combination of various helps. Some need job skills, some need to learn how to read and write, some need to end their substance abuse, some need medicinal aid to overcome depression. However, we all need the ability to love and respect ourselves, and to do this we need to acquire command of our own lives. Believe me, there is not one person who is repeatedly acting the part of a criminal who has command of his or her own life, and there is no criminal who has not gained a considerable degree of control of his or her own life who will ever be anywhere except on the verge of committing another crime. This is not an effort to be discouraging, just factual.

When I entered prison, I already possessed an education, job skills, mental health (as in brain chemistry) and physical health. However, I could not respect or love or even like myself, and I did not possess any self-command. All my plans lay subject to the arbitrary rule of my emotions, to the likes and dislikes of other people, and to the various compulsions that appeared at unexpected moments and ordered me away from meaningful activities to seek out power and sex and money and notoriety. What I needed from a rehabilitation program was the means to gain control of my own life. What I was offered by Vermont corrections was a way to intervene in the things which were still controlling my life. I was offered a box of bandaids for a reoccurring wound, not a way to stop being wounded.

My placement in the Federal Penitentiary at Lompoc, California was one of the best things that had ever happened to me. I was exposed to relatively normal people there. The drug dealers in Federal prison had not suffered the emotional damage many men in the state prison had. They were angry at the judicial system, but not at other people or the world in general. Most importantly, I became exposed to the Chapman University program at Lompoc. The education teachers in the Vermont prison system, well meaning as they were, had continually commented on how brilliant I was. However, when I began taking college courses, I found the Chapman University professors were not easily impressed.

The professors who came to the prison treated me like a person. It amazed me -- they weren't a bit afraid of me. I admired their courage and non-judgmental attitude. Theirs was not the challenging false courage I was used to encountering. The professors took the stance of: "We know there's something of value inside of you and if you don't destroy us in the process, we're going to help you retrieve it." They weren't frightened of being harmed; they were not offended by insults. I had never seen such self-command. For some reason, I knew it was the type of courage and self-command I had been searching for for a very long time.

One night I read a small book containing the description of a person whom I could only think detestable. In the morning, I awoke to the sight of the book laying on my nightstand, and I suddenly realized I was no different from the person described in the book. I gained a very clear view of my true self and I didn't like what I saw.

I met three other inmates who were also searching for a viable way to change their lives. I realized there were people more intelligent than myself in the world and that I may not be able to figure out how to straighten out my own life and become like the professors by my own methods. With these insights, I joined the three inmates I'd met in searching for methods that would have some real rehabilitative impact upon us. We were not searching for ways to look good, we were searching for ways to extinguish our hatred of ourselves and others, and to become truly self-commanding, courageous, self-respecting individuals.

After a few years in Federal prison in California, I was returned to state prison. When I was returned to Vermont, I was allowed to enter the Violent Offender program, a program designed to help people intervene in their violent behaviors. Unfortunately, prison policy soon changed and it was determined one could only enter a program while within two years of his minimum release date. Thus, I was stopped from completing that program.

Left to my own devices, I looked in other places to find ideas about how I could really change my life. I went to church, but the people there didn't have time to change their lives; they were too busy discussing what was wrong with other religions to study what was right about theirs. I started going to

Alcoholics Anonymous meetings; right away I found that many of the volunteers had all the attributes I'd previously observed only in the University Professors. Over time, I listened to many people who once had many of my own characteristics explain to me how they had changed their lives. Finally, I understood I needed to do many of the things they had done to see if they would work as well on myself.

What follows are, in a condensed version, the viewpoints I adopted, the actions I took and the results I obtained. I did not invent, develop or otherwise think of any of these viewpoints or methods; I just utilized them because of the liberty and serenity other people told me they'd derived from them.

1. I ended my drug and alcohol use. I did this by seeking those who had ended their own use of these substances and by doing what they told me they had done.

2. Instead of judging behavior, thought or speech as good or bad in a moral sense, I began to view and judge all personal conduct from the singular standpoint of whether it empowered me, debilitated me or concerned me at all. I am of the mind that conduct empowers me when it allows me to remain in reality and when it diminishes feelings of hostility and shame.

3. I came to understand that my ability to respect myself and therefore my ability to love myself rested not on an accumulation of wealth and skills and knowledge, but on the bedrock of appropriate conduct. How I choose to act determines whether or not I can respect and love myself. This was a radical idea! In one moment it changed my traditional thinking of 40 years from "what will or do they think of me" to "what do or will I think of myself?"

4. I differentiated hostility from anger. By hostility, I'm stating I intend to wage war and punish offending parties until they surrender or until I'm satisfied they've suffered at least as much as I have. Through the lens of hostility, I view people as enemies and disguise my cruelty as righteous. By anger, I am saying I disapprove of a particular behavior or event, and I intend to defend my goods, services, resources, serenity and security from theft, but I don't desire to punish the offending party. Through the lens of anger, I see victimizers as errant siblings in need of practicable methods to liberate themselves from the influence of a destructive lifestyle.

I looked back over all the years of my life and listed all the hostilities I still harbored towards various people, groups and institutions. I looked at what part I had played in the situations. I realized I have never gotten away with any mean or dishonest action without the consequence of increased hostility and of further reducing my control over myself, and that people who act with a hurtful motive suffer similar punishment. Lastly, I offered up all of my old hostilities to this system and got out of the punishment business.

5. I listed all the hostilities I harbored towards natural events and realized it was laughable for me to assume I was important enough for the natural world to single me out for special treatment. It was I who had been adopting goals and expectations in opposition to natural events.

6. I listed all the hostilities I harbored towards myself. I tried to think of everything I'd ever done or not done that would allow me to dislike myself, and I assembled a list of the negative character traits I'd exhibited, i.e. dishonesty, selfishness, etc. I came to understand that my destructive behaviors posed no lasting quality and were not as powerful as I'd liked to imagine, and I stopped equating criminal conduct with power.

7. I found someone with a closed mouth and a nonjudgmental nature and disclosed all the hostilities I'd listed against myself. As a result, recollections of the humiliating thoughts and behaviors lost their ability to emotionally disturb me to any great degree. That in itself was quite liberating.

8. I wrote down all the things I feared and collected them into categories. I found the vast majority of my fears pertained to my image, to the ways I'd wanted other people to view me. Others pertained to my hesitation to accept responsibility for my own choices, my dislike of unpredictable events and my view of success as unobtainable.

I combated my fears of other's thoughts about me by realizing people had better things to do than think about me. Further, I redoubled my efforts to stop using the opinions of other people as a source of self-respect. I moved instead towards the possession of personal character traits I, myself, could respect myself for. My quest for empowerment required me to find the courage to move onward to a lifestyle of reality, readily accepting blame for my own actions. I strove to recognize when I was blaming my own behavior on an outside source and to redirect my viewpoint. I discovered that my visions of success always contained the element of serenity. Unfortunately, I had been searching for serenity by collecting wealth, things, power over people and events, and by impressing others with my skills and intelligence. Working to acquire self-respect and reduce fear and hostility was instead the route to lead me to serenity. I combated my fears of unpredictable events by restraining myself from trying to control events I have no real control over and abandoning my efforts to predict the future to any great extent. I do plan for the future, but I concentrate on what I can do today to create the tomorrow I want. I have found that as long as I work to separate myself from the tools and deceptions of my old lifestyle, what the future delivers will always be better than what I'd had before.

9. I came to understand one cannot fully respect himself simply by acting in appropriate ways; one must also make reparation for past harmful conduct. Towards this end, I listed all the people, (including business owners and others effected by my behaviors), I had harmed in any way over my entire life. I reviewed each situation and estimated and noted the dollar figure of the monetary losses I'd caused others to suffer. Having completed my list, I wrote letters to every person and group I'd identified as having harmed. I apologized for my trespasses and accepted responsibility for my debts. Some of the smaller debts I paid right away, some will need to wait, some can be repaid in other ways. For example, I owe the taxpayers a large sum of money, but if I inspire one person to turn away from a life of crime, I will have repaid even this huge obligation.

10. I revisited the list of shame-producing character traits I'd assembled while exploring my hostility towards myself, and I assembled a list of character traits opposite to those I'd identified. I studied each character trait and made an effort to clarify what each meant to me. I was assembling a personal, moral base from which to direct my thoughts and actions.

11. I began a campaign to be helpful to others. This errand is as helpful to me as to others, because it lends my life a perceptible purpose and keeps my conduct appropriate; I would not be helpful if I demonstrated and modeled hurtful conduct.

12. I recognized that the cognitive and intervention strategies currently employed by Vermont corrections constitute wonderfully useful methods to maintain one's new lifestyle, after it is effected, and availed myself of the appropriate programs.

As a result of these actions I followed, my sessions of punitive self-hatred regarding my past actions have all but ended. My self-respect is no longer contingent upon what people think about me. I enjoy freedom from the futile labor of trying to persuade the world to conform to my will, and I seldom experience the necessity to try to convince anyone of anything or to change them. I possess no need to frighten people or to present myself as dangerous, crazy, hot tempered or intimidating. I've acquired the ability to form honest relationships with all types of people, and I welcome friendly relations, but it's no longer imperative I secure the friendship of any specific person. I seldom feel lonely and I no longer entertain thoughts of suicide. My life is as though I've stopped racing around a track and entered the calm of the infield. I can see people still struggling to outperform me and one another, but I no longer feel any need to be in the race. Life for me has stopped being a competition. I have come to understand there is nothing of value I can steal from people and no grand prize for being "the best." I enjoy a new ability to maintain my composure even while faced with difficult situations and confronted by the most obnoxious of people, no longer afraid that my emotions will force me to act destructively. I enjoy the liberty to use the wisdom and knowledge of yesterday's and today's people; this no longer threatens my independence and is a gift of incredible value to me.

Most important to me, by taking the actions I've described, my compulsions to commit crime have miraculously diminished to a point where a little willingness on my part easily keeps them at bay.

The thoughts pulling many convicted people toward destructive conduct are akin to the way excuses to smoke enter the mind of one who is trying to quit, or in line with the thoughts of a depressed individual who entertains the notion, "I should just kill myself," until he finally does try. These yearnings seem to emerge out of nowhere and become feared and ever-lurking opponents. Even knowing the almost certain consequences that follow destructive conduct are not enough to push the thoughts of it out of our minds. We are like the person who repeatedly tries to solve his problems by getting drunk, and discovering they are worse when he sobers, begins yet another drunken spree. Why does the alcoholic or cigarette smoker not just quit? Why does the overweight person simply stop eating so much food?

Those who say, "He could stop committing crimes if he really wanted to," are mistaken. Wanting to stop is not enough. Many people want to live normal, non-destructive lives, just as many people want to lose weight, stop smoking cigarettes and stop contemplating suicide. The program of Alcoholics Anonymous exists because people who wanted to stop drinking found they could not do so. Is anyone ready to tell the over two-million people in that organization that they hadn't really wanted to stop?

It is here I have good news for those who suffer as I did from recurring destructive thoughts. After taking the decisive actions I've described above, the thought of participating in destructive conduct has not overridden the command of my thoughts in three years. Before that time, I cannot remember three months passing in which destructive desires did not seize command of my thoughts. This new self-command is not unlike that enjoyed by the smoker who, years after quitting, may encounter the desire to smoke, but can now easily brush the thought aside. There are thousands of recovered alcoholics who had previously suffered from mental obsessions to drink. After doing their Twelve Steps, the obsession to drink was lifted.

I don't know why the methods I followed liberated me from the mental messages to be destructive. I didn't ask a "higher power" to do it. I just took the actions I've described and the destructive mental messages became infrequent and lost power over my self-direction. This strategy represents the missing link between Corrections' current cognitive and intervention strategies and long-term non-destructive conduct By turning criminal compulsions into the less intense form of a habit, the intervention and cognitive restructuring approaches then become viable rehabilitation strategies.

I could not have stayed out of prison before I took the actions I did. My emotions had been extremely unstable and I'd been consumed by hatred towards myself and others. I'd been addicted to alcohol and drugs and plagued by compulsions. I am none of these things now. Still, the lifestyle I lived for so long lurks, waiting for me to become so comfortable in my new lifestyle that I backslide. Even though I have built for myself a new style of living, I will need several things to stay out of prison when released. I will need to remain active in Alcoholics Anonymous to keep from returning to the use of alcohol, drugs and fantasy. I will need a support system in place, consisting of people I can be honest with without fear of them over-reacting. I will need to be sure I do not get involved in any co-dependent relationships -- to do this, I may need to forgo intimate relationships altogether. I will need to rebuild financial stability without getting caught up in the need to buy things, and I will need to remain active in doing voluntary service work to help others. Of course, I will need a job and an apartment, but I have never experienced difficulty with being employed or finding a place to live. I will need to maintain my new lifestyle by developing intervention techniques, and this is where it would be helpful to be involved in a group situation such as the programs many prisons utilize today, where other members of the group point out places one's thinking may yet be distorted and where intervention techniques are developed.

I have come a long way along a difficult route. It is as though I began what was supposed to be a constructive journey through life by first losing the equipment I needed to see me through. Then I found need to turn around, retrace the trail, pick up the gear and brush it off. Some of the equipment is bent and dented and can be patched up and used with care; some of the gear is damaged beyond repair. Nevertheless, I am now capable of moving forward. Today my life is filled with purpose and meaning and direction and power. I have been shown how to be of real help to people like myself. My life has become greatly simplified, and I have no desire to flee from reality or to act out the part of a criminal. Today, without resignation, apathy or undue effort, I've finally stopped hurting others and myself.

Calbraith MacLeod is a machinist by trade and has been a non-competitive bodybuilder since 1979. A native of Vermont, he has served over 17 calendar years in prison. He has spent time in five State Correctional Facilities, two Federal Penitentiaries and two Federal Correctional Institutions. During his incarceration, he has participated in numerous rehabilitation programs, including Vermont Correctional Industries Apprenticeship Program, Federal Drug and Alcohol Program, Thresholds, Vanguard, Vermont's early sex-offender program, the Violent Offenders Program, Cognitive Skills, Anger Management, the Productive Living Unit, Emotional Awareness and self-esteem groups. While incarcerated at the Federal Penitentiary at Lompoc, California, Cal participated in the Chapman University program and accumulated college course credits until he was returned to Vermont. He is currently serving a 40 year Vermont state prison term. Cal is the author of the book <u>Practical Reformation</u> (Audenreed Press) and is the rehabilitation editor for <u>CellDoor</u>, an internet magazine written by prisoners for free people.

THE TOP OF THE WELL

Diane Hamill Metzger

It's in these early hours of the morning when the virus of fear begins to multiply in my stomach. These stark hours, still quiet, when another day is about to begin. I can't explain why it is the morning and not the night that creeps in like an intruder and gets a hold of my throat. Perhaps it is because at night that protective blanket of darkness allows my mind to sneak away into fantasy where I am with my family, or driving down the highway, or sitting on a starlit beach with someone who loves me.

In my fantasies, I am free.

How do I describe a descent into hell and the slow, agonizing climb back out? Truth is, I'm not even back out yet, but I hope I'm getting closer. I keep trying to glimpse a light at the top of the well, something to let me know that it's going to be over eventually.

I came to prison at the age of 25 with no previous criminal record and a life sentence, co-defendant to my husband, a man twelve years my senior. I met him when I was only 18; by the time I was 20, we were married. He came with plenty of baggage: an ex-wife with whom he bickered constantly, children by that marriage and severe custody/child-support problems. I came with plenty of baggage of my own, not the least of which was a serious lack of self-esteem.

"Lack of self-esteem" -- you hear that so much now that sometimes it's considered a joke, a catch-word in the lexicon of "psycho-babble." But it's very, very real, and I believe that the lack of it accounts for a great majority of the social ills in this country, from the most miniscule to the most horrifying. Almost without exception, women in prison suffer from an overwhelming lack of self-esteem; at least they come in that way.

Most women doing time for homicide fall into two categories -- those who were accomplices in a crime of violence committed by a man, or those who killed an abusive spouse or boyfriend. Women usually don't commit random violence, multiple murders or rape-related killings; it is also rare for women to commit other crimes that include violence, (armed robberies, aggravated assault, etc.). Though a large percentage (75-80%) of women doing time are doing so for drug-related crime, (i.e. committing crime to get money to buy drugs), the crimes that women commit to support a drug habit are usually nonviolent in nature, such as forgery, shop lifting or prostitution.

This is still a man's world. Maybe, with our generation of "baby boomers" gaining some wisdom and passing it on to our children, things are beginning to change. But growing up, I never had any doubts about whose world it was. I knew at a young age that my father had wanted me to be a boy, so my first impression of myself was that I was a disappointment. My dad is from the "old school" where men are macho, girl-children are their mothers' responsibility, and fathers don't invest much emotion or affection in their little girls. I hold no animosity toward him; that was just the way things were back then, and my dad is a good man and a good provider. I know now that he loves me, in fact we've become very close. But growing up, all I felt was starved for male affection, attention and approval. And, as is so typical in so many females of my generation, I went looking for a "daddy" to love me.

I had another problem as well. I was not physically attractive, never the cutsie-pie cheerleader type. I was plain, athletic and a "brainiac," not exactly the type that attracted boys. Never mind that as compensation I became witty, creative, resourceful, compassionate and a good friend. None of these things brought me what I wanted most -- a boyfriend. Oh, now and then there would be a boy who liked me, who found that I was great fun to be with and who liked being with me. But inevitably, he'd get teased (more often than not by the girls) for being with a girl who wasn't pretty or part of the "in crowd," and he'd stop coming around. Girls can be terribly cruel to other girls and are often socialized to dislike and distrust one another. Where boys compete in sports and for career opportunities as well as dates, girls compete for just one thing and that's boys! So despite the fact that I was smart in school, talented in many areas and capable of getting into just about any college I chose, I wanted only one thing, the only thing that would make me a success in my own eyes -- a man to love me.

As a result, I chose not to go to college. In the year after I graduated from high school, I met the man who would become my husband. He was older, the father figure I'd been searching for, and intelligent, someone I could look up to. He was experienced and told me everything I wanted to hear. He said I was beautiful, something I'd never heard from a male in my life, and he told me he loved me. He was a dream come true. I would have done anything for him, anything to make sure he never left my life. I never saw that my husband's age, experience and intelligence allowed him to manipulate me in every way possible. I endured deceit and emotional abuse that I rationalized as necessary evils that every woman endures to keep her man. I knew, as a woman who would never be thought of as beautiful in a world where physical beauty is everything, I had to hold onto what I had, no matter how much pain went along with it.

It was at that point in my life that the unspeakable happened. On a summer night in 1974, while I and our six-month-old son were outside waiting in the car, my husband killed his ex-wife during a fight over child custody. The decisions that I made from that point on forever changed my life and the lives of the people I loved. I helped my husband in the attempted cover-up of what

41

he had done. My infant son and I were fugitives with him for nearly a year afterward, and when we were finally arrested, I made it very clear to the authorities that I would be telling them nothing. And they made it very clear to me that, as an uncooperative accomplice to my husband, under Pennsylvania's law of accomplice liability, I would be given a sentence identical to his, though I had done violence to no one. And that's exactly what happened. On the fateful day of my arrest, I was 25 years old. I am 50 years old now as I write this from prison where I have been for almost 25 years, serving a life sentence.

When I was arrested, my son was 17 months old. The night of our arrest by FBI agents in Boise, Idaho, my baby son was literally ripped, screaming, from my arms by a brusque child-welfare worker. I didn't see my son again for six months when my parents were finally able to wrest custody of him from a system eager to see him kept from me forever. Thus began years of seeing my son for only a few hours a month in prison visiting rooms, talking to him in cost-limiting 15-minute collect phone calls, and exchanging with him hundreds of letters that were opened and read by prison mail censors first. My son grew from a toddler to a schoolboy to a teenager to the adult man he is now, and I missed all of it. My parents gave him love, safety, security and all of his material needs, but they couldn't give him me.

My son and I have a loving relationship today, but not without much effort and much heartache. Who knows what our relationship could have been were we together all these years? Yet, as much sadness and regret as I feel about the loss of years with my son, I am relieved and grateful that my parents were there to raise him. So many children of incarcerated mothers tragically fall victim to the foster care system and are shifted from guardian to guardian. Their mothers in prison rarely, if ever, get to see them or form any relationship with them at all. It is agonizing for the mothers and their children and leaves both sides scarred forever. People should never assume that because a woman is in prison, she is a bad mother, that she doesn't love her children or that she doesn't deserve a loving relationship with them. A woman serving a life sentence in Pennsylvania endures a double-edged nightmare: that of doing a possibly endless sentence in prison, and that of knowing she may never be with her children again.

In Pennsylvania, all life sentences are without parole eligibility. Our only hope for freedom is via clemency and commutation of sentence from Pennsylvania's Board of Pardons and Governor. The past two decades in Pennsylvania have been ones of increasing "lock 'em up and throw away the key" hysteria, resulting in an almost automatic denial of commutations/ clemency for lifers. We can only hope that the new millennium brings with it a softening of the harsh attitudes that have robbed us of our hope.

The past two-and-a-half decades of my life have often been filled with anguish and despair, but they have also been ones of introspection, growth, maturation, learning and the acquisition of much wisdom. I often wonder if the passage of years outside would have brought me the degree and depth of these qualities that these years of imprisonment have brought me! I have been forced to face myself, to know myself and to learn to be true to myself. I have endured an environment of deprivation, regimentation and loss of personal freedoms that I always took for granted. I have had to co-exist in close quarters with people I thought to be so unlike myself that I couldn't imagine how I could share space and time with them. I have shed prejudices and gained understanding and empathy. I have found a courage within myself that I never knew I had. I have learned who and what are important in my life and have questioned everything that I thought I once believed. I have made such a concerted effort not to let the world go on without me that I am probably more aware and informed of the happenings in the world than many of the people out there living in it! I have educated myself to the most attainable degree possible within the confines of prison.

Some people look at me with pity and exclaim, "Oh, you've missed everything!" But I haven't, you see. I've missed many things, particularly the joy of physically being able to be there at events and with people. But I absorb everything from life that I can, from the TV, radio, books, newspapers, magazines and from the accounts of family, friends, acquaintances and strangers who relate to me the details of their lives and their experiences. I often live vicariously, but I live. I still feel the sun on my face and the wind in my hair as I walk from one building to another. The fences cannot deprive me of these things. I still write poetry, sing a song, laugh at a joke. There are days when despair threatens to envelope me, when I decry the loss of these years and yearn to hold a child, to pet a dog, to see and smell the ocean. Sometimes the abject need to be free and the overwhelming frustration of not being able to be almost swallow me up and the yearning is almost too much too bear. But I bear each sorrow one day at a time, knowing that the next day will bring a new joy, a new enlightenment, a new reason to be grateful for what I yet have.

My most fervent hope is to be free again, to enjoy my loved ones and to give back to them some of what they have so selflessly given me. My spirit can sometimes be bruised by those who feel that their job and duty and right is to punish, but my spirit is resilient and strong. No one yet has been able to crush it. I believe that the best restitution I can give to those I have hurt in this life is to live life the very best I can and to help anyone I can along the way, wherever I may be.

It's not ever easy. Make no mistake -- these walls are cruel. But each day I'm still making that climb out of the well to the top, one step and one day at a time. If I stop climbing, then those who wish to keep me encased behind walls have won. That won't happen.

I don't know what the future will bring. But I do know that I, and thousands of prisoners like me, fervently hope that the politicians and administrators and the people who live each day in society and take their freedom for granted will come to see that without the belief that people can

44

change, there can be no hope. Hope is the foundation upon which all life is built, that which allows us all to face each day with courage and positive anticipation.

Let there be hope for us all.

Diane Hamill Metzger is a Pennsylvania prisoner, born in 1949. She has been serving her life sentence since 1975, when her husband killed his ex-wife during a child custody dispute. Though she committed no act of violence, Diane assisted in the attempted cover-up of her husband's crime and was a fugitive with him until their arrest. Under Pennsylvania's law of accomplice liability, she was given a sentence identical to her husband's: life in prison. Diane's accomplishments during her incarceration are extraordinary. She has earned four college degrees, completed two apprenticeships, received citations from the Pennsylvania House of Representatives and Senate, and won numerous educational, literary and community-service awards. She is a published writer, poet and lyricist, and a member of MENSA and ASCAP. She works with at-risk juveniles from the community and says she considers her greatest accomplishments the times she is able to use her acquired wisdom to help a young person avoid making the mistakes that she did. Diane served the first 20 years of her life sentence in Pennsylvania, which still holds legal jurisdiction over her sentence and release. Since 1995, she has been serving her sentence in Delaware, where she was permitted to transfer in order to be closer to her son, parents and brother who are the lights at the top of her well.

AS THE WALLS CLOSE IN

Blake R. Pirtle

Entering this world, mortally innocent... I was thrust upon a cloud of insanity... Sights so strange, yet normal and unforbidding... To indulge in this insanity would be... To accept another world into the realms of my mind... Now the door is closed... I have escaped the universe, not to return until another life time... Locked in... Inside my own insane destiny... Which I have created... With no knowledge that I and only I... Am the holder of the key... To my destiny... To my sanity...

I am not your typical Death Row inmate; I just don't fit the mold. I come from a very stable childhood, have never been to prison before and never committed a violent crime before.

Yet my first violent crime landed me in prison and on Death Row. I was never given the second, third and sometimes fourth chances so many Death Row prisoners have received. And so here in prison for my first time is where I will die, one way or another. The only thing I feel I have in common with other Death Row inmates is the simple fact that I am a murderer. In the course of a robbery at the age of 23, I murdered two people I had known and worked with almost every day for over a year.

When trying to discover what in my life thrust me into this world, I cannot put my finger on just one event or circumstance. In the seven years I have been on Death Row, I have come to understand that there were a lot of causes and effects and chains of events that led me here and that there are no easy answers to my never-ending questions.

I was born the eighth of 11 children. We lived in a big white house in one of the best neighborhoods in Spokane, Washington. We had the white picket fence, a big yard with lots of grass, two apple trees and an apricot tree, a driveway with a basketball hoop on the garage and a big old park only one block away. As a child, I had all the toys I ever wanted, new clothes for school every year, always a bicycle, and we had motorcycles and a place at the lake to spend the summer months, complete with a skiboat, water skis and everything a kid could want to make his time at the lake as fun as it could possibly be.

I grew up with two involved and committed parents. My father was a "man's man" who worked his whole life to provide for his family. He taught us to hunt and fish, ride motorcycles, work on our bikes and how to build or fix just about anything. He did not believe in allowances and taught us a very strong commitment to work. He always made us understand not to get caught up in what people thought or said about us. But my father was also a very complicated man, for the only emotion he ever showed was anger. He was impossible to get close to. He was very strict and used to discipline us in extreme ways that most people nowadays would say was abusive. My father's fault as a man was that he was extremely violent and felt the need to make everyone fear him. And we did! We always did our chores on time and walked on egg shells around him for fear of putting him in a bad mood.

My mother was a housewife and a very loving and giving woman. She was always there for us when we came home from school or were sick or hurt. She always made sure we had good meals, clean clothes and a clean house. There was nothing she would not do for her children. Because of that, she suffered a lot of abuse from my father, for she would step in when he was disciplining us. With my dad, that was the wrong thing to do, for women had no say. As strict as my father was, my mother was just the opposite. She was soft and easy, would let us children get away with stuff and keep our misbehavior from my dad. It was a terrible combination for us kids. We picked up on it and knew that if we got in trouble, didn't do well in school, etc., Mom would protect us.

Despite my parents' differences, looking back on this, I really cannot understand what happened to me. All ten of my other brothers and sisters have very normal lives -- so what happened to Blake?

Being the eighth child of eleven, I learned that it was very easy to go unnoticed in my family. So I started to do things to get noticed, a lot of them good, some bad -- it just didn't matter as long as I got the attention I was looking for. I might fight with my brothers or get caught shop lifting, not do my chores or stay out on my bike all day and miss dinner. Or I might clean my room extra well and show it off to my parents, get up early and make everyone breakfast, follow my father around all day doing odds and ends for him, help my mother with all her household duties, or spend all summer mowing lawns and all winter shoveling sidewalks, saving my money and buying everyone in my family silly little Christmas gifts. I was a child who needed to be noticed!

My first introduction into the world of crime was through drugs. I can still remember it as clearly today as the day it happened. My brother Jay is five years older than me and he was someone I looked up to. I idolized him and his friends, always trying to hang out with them and do the things that they did. But because of the age gap, as you can imagine, I was not always welcome in their group.

One Sunday morning during the summer between third and fourth grade, (I must have been about eight years old), Jay and I had the chore of cleaning the basement of our house. As we were down there cleaning, we saw a stray cat in a crawl space. The day before we had seen a sign on the corner telephone pole offering a reward for a lost cat and we were sure that this was the one. We spent the next six hours of the day under our house trying like hell to catch that poor cat. At last we did; it was the lost cat and we received a $15 reward from the owners. My father made us give five dollars to my mom for all the clothes we'd dirtied up, but the rest was ours to do with as we saw fit.

Like I said, my dad did not believe in allowances, so any money we earned was ours to spend any way we chose. My brother Jay talked me into buying some marijuana with him. I quickly agreed because I idolized him and didn't want to seem like a child, so we bought some pot and smoked it in the park. I can remember that that first time it didn't do anything for me, but I was happy because Jay and I shared a secret and I was now allowed to hang around with him and his friends because I now smoked pot and drank with them. This was at the age of nine or ten, during the fourth grade. Now when Jay and his friends partied, I was always there. They thought it was funny to see me stoned out of my mind and falling down drunk, and I was more than pleased to do it, for it provided me the attention I so desperately needed. We would all get drunk and stoned, vandalize stuff around the neighborhood and steal whatever we wanted to.

My introduction to the criminal justice system was one of the scariest things I ever had to deal with. My parents never knew of my problems and I never got caught at anything until the summer between the sixth and seventh grades. We were at the lake for the summer and Jay stayed in Spokane because he had a job. I broke into one of the neighbor's cabins and stole a whole bunch of fishing poles and tackle boxes. I don't know what I planned to do with them, but I wanted them. I cut my arm really badly going through the broken window. When the police showed up a few days later, they pretty much knew it was me because of the cut on my upper arm and the blood in the cabin. I was a good liar by this time and told them I had cut myself on the dock. The police did not believe me, but how could they prove this was not the truth?

Well, later that day, my mom found the stolen goods where I had hidden them and she turned me in. To the surprise of everyone, the police came and took me away. I was taken to the jail in Newport, Washington and placed in a solitary cell, for they did not have a juvenile area. The police had no intentions of booking me and releasing me to my parents; they kept me in their jail, at the age of 11, for the whole weekend until I could go before the judge. This was probably the worst thing they could have done, for it destroyed my mother. She thought she had done the right thing and here they were taking her baby away from her. She would never again turn me in to the police and would do everything she could to protect me from them.

Later that summer, I was sentenced in Spokane to 30 days in Juvenile for breaking into that cabin, so I started the seventh grade on school release from Juvenile. By the middle of seventh grade, I was doing speed, smoking pot everyday and drinking whenever I could. I started selling pot and speed in school that year too. And for the next four years, I was in and out of Juvenile more than I like to admit. On top of selling drugs at school, I became a big time thief, for a child that is. I would sneak out at night and break into people's houses, garages, cars, whatever suited me. On top of that, I would sneak out to go to my brother's parties. So many nights as a child, I would find myself stumbling home drunk and out of my mind, trying to climb up that damn apple tree to get back in my window.

I quickly developed a comfort zone for being locked up. I learned how to

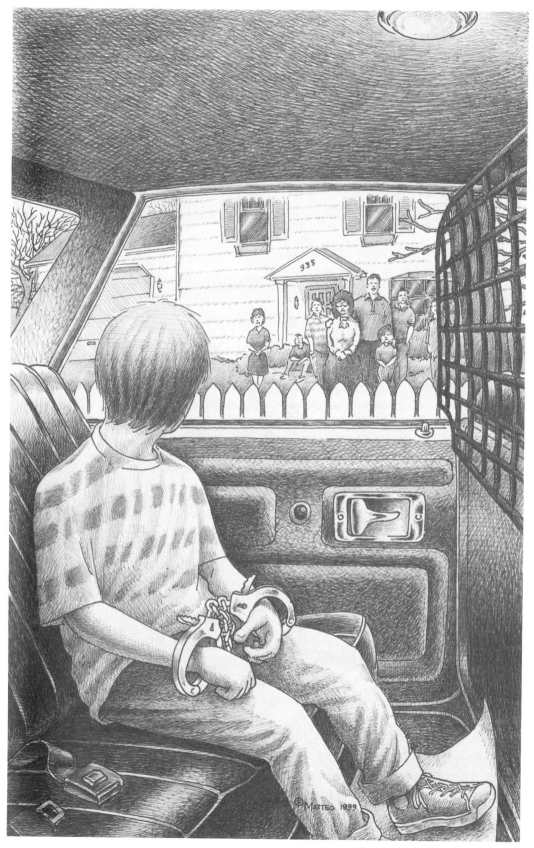

use the system to where all I really did was sleep there. I had school release, drug programs to go to, community service, etc. On top of that, I built up a huge tolerance to the drugs I was doing; combining that with my ability to lie, no one could see my problem, plus I was getting all the attention I wanted. In Juvenile, they were putting me through every program they could think of to try and solve my problems. I got all kinds of attention from my older brothers and friends, for they all thought it was cool that this little kid could drink and smoke as much as they could. At home, I got more attention than my brothers and sisters, for I was the only one of them in constant trouble. I don't believe I did all of this just for the attention or for the need to buy drugs. I think that more than anything I found an extra thrill in my crimes, a high in itself.

Junior High and High School were a total waste for me. I made it through the 11th grade, but never learned a thing. I was there, but I assaulted my mind with so much speed and pot that there was no way I could learn anything. The only things I was interested in were drugs, sex and partying!

I stopped committing thefts in the 10th grade at the age of 15, because the last time I was busted and sentenced, the Judge looked me in the eye and told me this was the last time -- next time no Juvenile, you are going across the mountains to the Institution. I believed him, so stopped doing crime, for no matter how comfortable I was doing time, I didn't want any part of the Institutions far from home. Besides, I didn't have to steal to make money. I made enough selling pot and speed to support my needs. School was my avenue for that and I could always do odd jobs around my neighborhood, right? Well, not anymore. I had stolen from so many people and had been taken away from my house by the police so many times that no one trusted me anymore. Whether I was doing crime or not, I was always going to be labeled a thief.

So I went to school to sell drugs, meet girls and find out where the parties were. My parents were not strict about good grades as long as we passed. How I lasted until the 11th grade I'll never know, but they kept passing me along, even though I later found out that I had very few credits.

Although I was no longer breaking the law by doing crimes on the streets, I was still breaking it by selling drugs and using them. I no longer felt the need to be noticed, for my drug use had taken over. I got to the point that the only time I felt normal was when I was high. I used to say, "I don't get high, I get normal," and that really was the truth, for I now felt completely unable to function if I was not high. I would smoke pot from the time I woke up until I went to bed. I would take a handful of speed every morning, drink whenever I could and was extremely sexually active. It was almost comical, considering all the shit I was doing in school, (drugs, drinking, sex, skipping class, fighting, selling on campus, etc.), because you know what I finally got kicked out of school for? Chewing tobacco!

Now, I don't think that it's funny that a 16 year old kid gets kicked out of school for good with no more chance for an education, but sitting here on Death Row for the past seven years, trying to pinpoint things in my life that led me down the path I chose, I do have to smile at what got me kicked out of school. It's not like they didn't have a clue that I was doing a lot worse things. I was skipping class all the time and, when I was there, I was completely doped up on drugs. They knew all the other shit that was going on in my life, but refused to address the problem.

Well, getting kicked out of school was no big deal in my household. My parents were not real strict about us doing well in school, plus by then I had my first job at a local hotel, so I just went to work full-time. At this point in my life, I was no longer committing crimes, but I was still using drugs very heavily and drinking a lot. I never considered this a crime, for it had been such a normal part of my everyday life for so long. By now I had gotten myself into hallucinogens, using them every chance I got, but I was still making my own money and not getting into trouble. I had a steady girlfriend and my first car.

But that summer, the summer of 1985 when I was 17, my whole world was about to change. My father got a job in Montana and was moving the whole family there. Well, I wasn't going to go; I was in love, had a good job, a car, etc., so my dad told me to find a place to live. I did. I moved in with my older sister for the next six months and in that short amount of time, I was successful in losing my job and my teenage love. I found a new job easily enough, for I was and still am a very hard worker, but losing my first job was a warning I did not see, for I had been fired for stealing alcohol.

I moved out of my sister's house in the spring of 1986 and got my own apartment. My whole family was in Montana, so I was pretty much alone to do what I wanted. And I did -- a lot of partying and, instead of buying the things I needed to furnish my apartment, I found an easier way. I made a trip out to the lake where I knew there were a ton of furnished trailers and I stole all the things I needed. Then I was introduced to harder drugs in the form of cocaine. Very quickly, I started freebasing cocaine, that is cooking it up into rock form and smoking it. I quickly lost my job, but just as quickly found a new one, my third one in two years. I lost my apartment, because I was spending all my money on cocaine, but I found a new place to live -- with my brother, for he had moved back to Spokane from Montana. My brother Trevor rarely used drugs, so I thought that this would be a good influence for me. It was not; I was set in my ways and was going to do whatever made Blake happy.

I went from cocaine to heroin in a matter of weeks, then to the needle, something I had always told myself I would never do. Heroin scared the piss out of me for I loved it and I did not mind injecting the needle at all, plus it was the only drug that left me physically sick when I was unable to use it. In a span of 30 days, I lost my job (for guess what -- yes, stealing), lost my apartment and just about everything I owned. I swore myself off of heroin after using it for about five weeks, but I stupidly replaced my need for a high by freebasing cocaine again.

For the next six years I was a very sick person. By the age of 17, I had tried every drug you could think of. I bounced around from job to job; I could never keep one for any length of time, for I couldn't stop stealing from the people I worked for. I was always in and out of jail for theft and different property crimes, nothing ever too serious. And I never lived in a place for over six months for I would never pay my bills.

The drugs truly controlled me. Of course I couldn't see it at the time, but I would steal from anyone, just as long as I was able to get my next fix. I would never hurt anyone in a physical sense, and at times I would do well -- get off the drugs, hold down one of my many jobs, get healthy, stay out of trouble -- but it never lasted. The need to fry my mind with drugs always took over and I was right back into the same bullshit.

In 1991, I got out of jail. I had done 8 months and I swore this was my last time and I was going to do good. I quickly got a job and found a place to live; it was a total dump, but I only had to pay $100 a month for a three-bedroom house because the landlord expected me to do a lot of the work to fix it up, which I did nonstop. I was able to buy myself a pretty decent used car, had a new woman in my life and she was pregnant with my second son. I was still using pot, speed and alcohol, but these were such an everyday part of my life that they didn't affect the way I lived. Remember, I didn't get high, I got normal! I refused to use cocaine and I was doing well.

In March of 1992, my life was the best it had ever been. Alice was a little over three months pregnant with my child, I was working steadily, in love, had a car and a nice house to live in. Then on March 22nd, I got a call early one morning that my dad had died -- a massive heart attack in his sleep. It was the first death in my large family. All I could remember about my father after his death were all the bad things.

When my dad died, I was filled with so many conflicting emotions; I was hurting, I was angry, I was sad and my heart was shattered. There were so many things I felt in need to talk to him about and now he was gone. So I took a page out of his book and held everything inside, letting no one know I was dying inside, and my life fell apart.

I tried like hell to do away with what I was feeling through alcohol and drugs, but all that did was add to my anger and pain and send me down the path of total destruction. In preparing for my trial for double murder, my anger and hurt were multiplied 100-fold, for all anyone did was concentrate on the bad things about my father and my childhood. If you would have asked me right after my trial, I would have said I had the worst life possible and everything I did in life was my parents' fault!

It took me three or four years in prison to accept my own faults and mistakes in life. Once I was able to do that, I was able to accept all of my father's shortcomings and I was once again able to see and acknowledge all the good he did.

A lot of people are amazed that I can now say that my father was a loving father. Well, it is the truth; there was never sexual abuse in my life and I still say to this day that my father's biggest faults as a man and father were the fact that he was violent and beat my mother, and his need to make everyone around him fear him. Not once in my life did I ever see anyone stand up to my father. I do believe now that the worst thing my brothers and sisters and I had to deal with growing up was watching my mother get beat up whenever she tried to stick up for us kids. Plus there was the mental stress my dad inflicted on us. He went out of his way to make us fear him and show us there was no way we could hurt him. I still remember some of the things he did, like sticking a straight pin through one side of his wrist and pulling it out the other side with a pair of pliers, pulling his own teeth out and always making us watch, just so we would know that pain did not affect him.

I can and do forgive my father for everything in life except the way he treated my mother, for in my eyes that is unforgivable, but I can now remember his gentle lovingness. Like the time my baby sister was in a terrible accident and had to have three brain surgeries; the doctors told my parents all they could do now was pray. I was being a little asshole because I was not getting the attention I needed and was refusing to go see my sister. It was the closest I ever saw my dad to crying when he sat me down and explained to me that this could be the last time I ever saw her. There was the time I was in the sixth grade and cut the tip of my finger off. By God, I was going to be a man like my dad and I was not going to cry. I didn't either, but I was scared to death! My father would not leave the operating room; he stayed there the whole time holding my good hand, talking to me and making sure I never looked at what the doctors were doing.

I can now remember my dad for the excellent teacher he was; it's what he did for the last 20 years of his life. He taught people like me, ex-cons, men and women with nothing else in life going for them, how to finish cement, placed them in the Union and got them good paying jobs. He did that in Spokane for 10 years and then for the next 10 he taught it in the Job Corps in Montana. I always thought he was a jerk when he was making us learn something from him, but now I see that he was just taking the time to teach us the proper and right way to do things in life.

The biggest example of my dad's love and caring that I always took for granted when I was free was that his home was always open to me. No matter how many times I screwed him over, ripped him off or just did wrong by him, I could always show up at his doorstep unannounced. No matter what, there was always a place for me to sleep and food for me to eat for as long as I needed to be there, no questions asked. How many kids can say that about a father they stole from left and right almost all their lives?

I still remember the last conversation I had with my dad. To this day, when I think about it, eight years after his death, it still breaks my heart. It was the closest he ever came to showing me he actually felt emotion. It was six months before his death; I had gone to Montana to visit him and he was so excited. He was counting down the days to his retirement -- eight months and counting! He told me as we were talking about it, "Son, I worked all my life and now for once I will be able to do whatever I want to do, no more bosses. I can sleep until noon if I like, go camping or hunting whenever I want for as long as I like, whatever tickles my fancy." This was said with the biggest smile I had ever seen on my father's face. I was so happy for him! We buried my father five months later, 90 days before he was due to retire.

After his death and then the loss of my car, job and Alice, pregnant with my son, I just lost it. Late in April of 1992, when I was asked if I wanted to try some crystalmeth (crank, a methamphetamine), I said why the hell not -- it's just a form of speed and I've been doing that all my life; I can control it. Well, it's the purest form of speed and I couldn't control it at all. Within weeks I was addicted, and soon was using the needle to get the most out of it. In May of 1992, I had been using it pretty steadily and I went on a rampage for seven days straight, using as much as I could, getting maybe eight hours of sleep every four days or so. I don't know if I can explain the effects of this to the average reader, but this shit wires you out; you are bug-eyed and always on the move. And when you abuse it at the level I did, you start to hallucinate from the lack of sleep and food and constant use of the drug.

This is the state I was in early Sunday morning on the 17th of May when I put a kitchen knife in my pocket and decided to go rob the last place I had worked. I had never used a weapon in any of my crimes, but on that morning, I walked into that restaurant and not only robbed it, but, in a delusional state of mind, killed two people I had known and worked with for over a year.

After seven years, I still have no idea what truly took place that morning. I have no answers. All I know for sure is that I murdered two people. I am now on Death Row for my first violent crime, and life as I know it is over forever. But did I ever really live? I don't know; all I know is that I was never a violent person and I'll never know what triggered me to do what I did. Often, in my seven years of life on Death Row, I've gone over my life, trying to pinpoint things that I could have done differently. I do believe now that I was doomed from a very early age. I was so young when I was introduced to drugs and crime that I convinced myself it was perfectly normal.

Now don't be mistaken -- when I was a juvenile, they put me through every program they could think of: drug rehab, counseling, probation, etc. But nothing worked, for by then I had become a very accomplished liar and would say all the right things until the heat was off me and I could dive right back into the same shit. But just maybe if my brother had not introduced me to drugs at the age of eight; maybe if my family wasn't so big and my parents had noticed me more; maybe if my father was not so strict or didn't beat my mother or insist on making everyone fear him; maybe if my mother wasn't so easy, if she had not written me notes when I skipped school or tried to protect me from my father's strict discipline. Yes, these all played a role in my life and the choices I made, but I was the one who made those choices. I took the path I did and I am responsible for my actions.

I often think about what would help kids in the same boat I was in back then and it is a very hard question indeed! My advice would be to parents, teachers and any other adult figure in that child's life: be involved in their lives, know what they are doing, recognize the patterns of trouble for what they are. Don't accept their lies, for they will lie their asses off. Surround them with positive things, constructive things. Be their friend, but be strict with them, talk with them and just always be there for them to have someone to come to. Stop at nothing to straighten out the child's life. Sometimes tough love is the best.

My advice to the kids dealing with these problems is pretty basic. You have got to want to change if you don't like the things you are doing with your life. Go to your parents, a teacher or other adult and tell them everything you're doing -- the drugs, sex, crime -- and that you need their help. I do believe that most adults would do anything to make a kid's life better, but if you don't go to them, open up to them, trust them and are willing to do whatever it takes to change, if you hold it all in and just try to deal with your life like I did, all too soon that life will seem very normal to you and you will end up just like me. You may not become a killer, but the chances are pretty good you will land your ass in prison!

I do believe that most of the responsibility falls on the adults' shoulders; parents, teachers, aunts, uncles have to be role models to kids and be aware of the things they are into. My parents let me fall through the cracks of life, though not intentionally. They just never took notice of all the bad things I was doing. They had no idea of the level of drug abuse I was into; they had no idea I would sneak out of the house at the age of 13 and go to my brother's parties. When they did catch me doing stuff, they were too trusting and believed my lies. And I don't have a clue what they thought when I kept getting into trouble with the law and landing in Juvenile. Maybe they felt I was just seeking attention, which was true, but if they were aware of the level of drugs I was doing, they would have known I had a much more serious problem.

Since I have been on Death Row, I am always asked what the prison system and Department of Corrections could do to give inmates a better chance at making it outside of prison. I believe that the first problem is that inmates have to want to change and become better men and women. Without that desire, very few will. The biggest problem I see with inmates is that so many have no education or job skills. All they know is crime. Many have never held down a steady job, had to pay rent, buy their own food, pay bills, wash their own clothes or meet any other responsibilities of everyday life. So there are a lot of things that the prison system can do to give inmates a fighting chance on the outside. And they better do something soon. If not, more and more prisons will be built and they will fill up very fast.

The prison system is failing because there is no such thing as rehabilitation these days. Inmates do their time, then we are let loose, right back into the same communities we came from, right back into the same circuses that sent us here. Crime is our only skill, so even if we want to change, we have no real chance at being successful.

I believe the change has to start with education. The system needs to provide all inmates with a chance at a proper and formal education and the ones that want to change will take full advantage of it. The next step I believe the system should take is to provide jobs and job training. So many have no job skills at all and no understanding of working a 40 hour week. Without that, how can any inmate go out and expect to get and hold down a reasonable job? How can we accomplish this? I have a very simple idea.

There are so many companies out there like Nike who manufacture their products in other countries because of cheap labor. Well, we have one of the biggest, cheapest labor forces right here in the USA -- prisoners in prison. These companies could be encouraged to set up industries in prisons across the country and hire prisoners at a very cheap rate. You could pay inmates $10/day and make it mandatory that 70% of their pay be saved for their release. Not only would inmates be leaving here with money to get started, but they would be receiving valuable job training and work skills. I also believe that the government needs to start encouraging companies to hire ex-felons. They could be given benefits and tax breaks for participating in a program like that. It is extremely hard for an ex-convict to find employment; most companies will not take a chance on him at all, so let's make it hard for them to refuse taking the chance.

On top of that, I believe we need to set up a relocation program for inmates. We have to quit sending these people right back into the same environment that helped put them in here in the first place. I will use myself as an example. I came to prison knowing nothing but crime and drugs for all my life. I would leave prison with an education and job skills. I would be sent to a new state with enough savings to rent an apartment, buy clothes, furnish my apartment and maybe get a car. I have a job which begins in a week at the local construction company at a decent salary without facing discrimination about the mistakes I made in the past. What are the odds I'll make it and do well? Very high! I have a whole new start plus a positive self-image, for I now have a trade, education and funds to be able to support myself.

I'm not stupid enough to believe that this would work for all inmates, because the sad truth is that for a lot of inmates nothing will work to change them. And I know that the public would probably go nuts over a program like this. I can just hear it now: "We're providing education, job training and jobs for total screw-ups!?" But, people, we have to do something soon to give inmates being released from prison a chance to become responsible, law-abiding citizens. What kind of country would you rather live in -- one that gives ex-felons hope and a fighting chance at a life outside of prison, or one that uses billions of your tax dollars to house 20-30 million prisoners across the United States? If things don't change for the better and soon, that is what our country will be facing.

Blake Pirtle *is now, for the first time he can remember, straight and sober. "I am truly amazed at what the mind, body and man is capable of when not polluted by drugs and alcohol." His goal is to strive each day to be a better brother, uncle, father, friend, son, nephew, writer and all-around man. His poetry has been published in <u>Trapped Under Ice: A Death Row Anthology (Biddle Publishing)</u>. Blake has been on death row in the state of Washington for eight years and his case is still under appeal. It is his hope that his sentence of death with be reversed to that of life without parole.*

SOME INDISTINCT WHITE NOISE

Joseph Burgeson

Nothing But the Truth

I wasn't convicted of killing a cop,
nor am I a black hurricane,
but rather some indistinct white noise.
Mine was not a famous case taken up by celebrities,
though I admit to a bit of local notoriety.
Also to being guilty as hell.
The only controversy over my arrest
was why the devil I was let out again in the first place.
I'm expendable, dispensable, disposable,
the wrong color for social causes and salvation,
no excuses allowed,
the right color for a high-number plea bargain
with a swift kick in the ass to seal the deal.
Being white and not a rat will get you tacitly singled out,
 beginning of sentence, end of sentence, period.
It's safe to mete us out the harshest,
really, what are we going to cry, racism?
and who will fight for our truth??
Right, excuse you while you fall down laughing.
Mothers may weep for lost sons,
but whales, test animals, owls, even trees
are better causes than we are.
No, no cause fighting for me.
Did I already say I was guilty?

A Letter

An envelope slides under my cell door with a soft swish,
the whispered announcement of a letter's arrival.
In an instant the welcome lightness
of its paper symmetry is in my hands,
a sudden gift I can't wait to open.
It's her.
My heart quickens
for the hopes taking prominence in rapid succession:
(she still loves me the lawyer says it looks good the family
        will visit soon...)
As I unfold the pages
her thoughtful essence emanates from them;
for a heady moment she's there,
close as I breathe,
a rose whose blush
puts blood back into the face of my humanity
as I forget for a while.

No More Rewinds

He was from Boston, where
he'd testified against his own brother
and gotten him 99 years plus life.
He eventually wound up here where he was safe,
everyone knowing Connecticut guys are soft.
Swaggering around with the homo
he was cheating on his wife with and
talking about going home,
he was run through with a sword
at breakfast one morning,
his blood shooting so far out in front of him
that he was stepping in it as he ran.
Collapsing in the hall he lay there on his side,
putting his hand to his chest and
staring in dumb amazement
at the gushes of his life, God, so much of it
you could smell it, like wet pennies,
his heart pumping it out generously
in its final betrayal.
Rogers the guard, crew-cut hard and quietly mean
in his hatred of cons, kneeling beside him,
crying, asking him if he was Catholic or Protestant,
telling him urgently to pray, pray, <u>pray!</u>
I stood there watching his dying,
Rogers telling me to get the hell away but I wouldn't,
wanting to see. I've never seen such human
sadness in a face, his eyes looking
at the winter morning sunlight shining
through the windows, and something else there,
a sense of him trying to rewind events, reality
back, back to not get up for breakfast that morning,
start the day all over, no, oh God no, why me,
quick, hurry,
back to the manly prisons he didn't get killed in,
to his wife, his mother, his brother,
rewind it back and back
to the beginning,
not now, please,
slowing,
back . . .

Rogers never came back to work again.

Concrete Genius

If I pronounce philosophical certainties,
they are my certainties.
And I'm a hypocrite.
Sometimes I love what I always hate.
I deftly turn the pages
of great men's minds,
dissecting the heart of their knowledge
with the keen edge of my intellect,
thinking what a clever surgeon I am.
Perhaps I'm only cutting down trees.
The eco-nuts wouldn't like that,
but what do they know?
At times all I know is that I'm in this cell.
I'm certain of that.

Beautiful

He's a study in tense mannerisms,
seemingly never relaxed.
Standing and watching
or sitting playing cards,
his head's always moving
this way then that,
eyes narrowed and brows knit,
missing nothing.
Even when he's still he's emitting energy,
bunched and tightly coiled,
ready.
When he was a toddling boy
his mother loved him tenderly and dearly
in his beautiful innocence,
unaware of the abuse
or the effects of violence
on a child's developing brain.
Not knowing, she couldn't protect him.
After thirty years of acting out
the anger and violence
that disordered his young mind,
he's been designated career criminal
and discarded.
Yet humanity and decency
still live in his soul,
and if caught at a moment
when he's smiling his mother's smile
it can be seen there,
shining in the eyes
of the man's little boy
who anger beat on
but couldn't destroy.

No Passage

I hate that door. It's open when I'm out and locked when I'm in. Sometimes I kick it. Cold steel, dull, unyielding, indifferent. Not like wood. Wood has heart and resiliency, resounding with its own natural character when struck. Like a wooden door, I was once alive. And, too, I am set upon a threshold, neither going in or coming out. My life passes through me and doesn't take me with it. I hate myself that door. Sometimes I kick it.

Looking In Looking Out

The flickering screen plays across his face,
bathing him in a pale light
while casting shadowy figures
on the perimeter of his campfire fixation.
He's as gone in his getaway
as an escaped convict,
but there's no pursuit
because only his mind is missing
in that little box.
The guard making his rounds
views the same scene
in cell after cell, reassured
that each bad actor is securely tuned in.
There's one, though,
looking out his remembering window,
pensively watching the moon tide the night.
He makes the guard uneasy,
this one thinking in the dark.

Mail Man

Wyatt Earp's coming down the tier, passing out mail.
Got a bullet with my name on it.
His creep shoes squeak at my door.
"Mail!"
As I head for the door he laughs a gotcha laugh.
I look at him.
Hate.
We stare, right and fight,
til he withers and leaves,
my eyes following,
staring,
glaring,
tearing to pieces,
a straight razor frenzying his picture.
I set the pieces on fire.
I piss on the ashes.
No mail again.

Staying

The lighthouse stands firmly on the point,
anchored by the seascape
to wash amid the oceaning sky.
Landmark for mariners and landsmen alike,
its graceful white beauty
is silent and powerful,
conveying a solid permanence that reassures,
that says, "I am here."
Coming into view it greets me
like a waiting friend,
calling my mind to familiar shores
of home and childhood summers,
bidding my faring heart
stay a while
where light's the best on returning.

Laid to Rest

It was actually snowing on Christmas Eve.
Snug, insular, and fitting.
I hummed Joy to the World
as I hung the last of my hand-made paper ornaments
in the otherworldly home of my cell,
which if nothing else was warm.
A passing guard noticed what I was doing and,
the righteous vengeance of his job offended,
decided to correct my attitude in his spirit of the season
by searching my cell.
As he poked around and threw things about,
his yuletide carol sang out,
--you can't have this, that will have to go, ho ho ho--
then he crumpled and crushed my delicate decorations
in his indignant exception,
and confiscated my soap-carved Christmas tree
I'd sprinkled with green and red glitters.
With triumph in his eyes and spiteful glee in his smile,
he told me he was writing me up for cell violations,
and wished me a Merry Christmas.
I got a lump in my throat the size of a piece of coal,
because I knew what he was doing and couldn't stop him;
he was stealing the little boy's Christmas.
He knew the boy was the only one who still cared.
As the boy wept silently at the unfairness of it,
I killed him because I loved him
and buried him forever.
The guard went home after his shift justified,
probably kissed his wife under the mistletoe,
opened gifts with his children,
drank some egg nog,
then settled down for a long winter's nap.
I went to bed and lay awake all night,
his malicious grin in my stocking
and visions of his dead family dancing in my head.

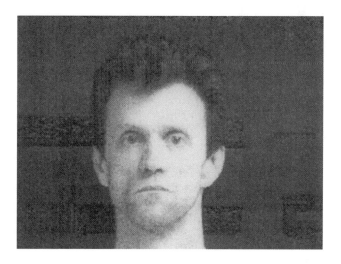

Joseph Burgeson *has spent most of his adult life in prison. He was a criminal and then an addict for most of that. He's no longer either. Growing up in New Haven, Connecticut in a very violent home, he was first sent away at age 13. He's now 44. Through the process of recovery and self-examination, together with his faith, he has overcome himself in the last three years and grown into a human being, a person. It's the hardest thing he's ever done, harder even than all the time he's done, and it's work still in progress. Joe has a rage, a sensibility and a talent to express them that enables him to write poetry.*

THE METAMORPHOSIS: HOODLUM TO BUTTERFLY

Willie Christopher Tucker

Most of the events described in this essay are very personal and yet profoundly universal. The issue of family cohesiveness and steadfastness is one that has troubled my family all of my life. But there has always been that "beacon of light," the fulcrum on which our family stands -- my mother Ruby. She is indeed a sustainer, provider and a beautiful person. I now write these excerpts from the pages of my life; I do so under the real threat of retaliation, but I have no fear. Because what is life without having dared to live? I hope that my brother Mark reads this and that we can break the ten years of bitter division and silence. To my family with love -- Willie

When I was first asked to participate in this project (Frontiers of Justice: Volume 3), I wrote an essay which was full of statistics and the usual rehabilitation jargon used when discussing prisoners and their possible reintegration into an angry society. But after some consideration, I knew it wasn't what I truly wanted to say. It was politically correct, but lacked several key components which are essential -- specifically, heart and truth. There are already enough robotic writings on prison reform, so I decided to focus on myself, my experiences. It's not a Norman Rockwell, in fact it's not a very pretty picture at all. It is a portrait of the misunderstood, all-American, ghetto youth. It is also a story of endurance, courage and personal triumph. Maybe what I have to say will help someone else heal their own wounds.

I can remember back as far as three or four years of age, growing up fast in the housing projects of Atlanta's west side. Dr. Martin Luther King Jr. had recently been assassinated, yet it was a miraculously powerful time for African-Americans here in the United States. Everyone I knew was extremely poor, but it didn't matter because everybody was experiencing black pride. James Brown blasted from front porch speakers, "Say it loud, I'm black and I'm proud." Adults were respected, and no matter who your parents were or whose child you were, if you were seen doing something wrong, you were punished on the spot by whomever caught you. It didn't matter if it was a blood relative or Ms. Odessa from down the street. If you did something wrong, you were set straight. The community was one unit and people cared enough to get involved.

But I guess that just wasn't enough. Those early years were spent mostly fatherless, for me as well as for most of my friends. We kind of taught each other about life, you know, in a kid sort of way. The streets of the projects were our fathers. The drunks, the drug dealers, the pimps, the addicts -- they were what we saw day in and day out. They were the only people who would take a moment out of their busy schedules to talk to us and give us a friendly, or sometimes not so friendly, word of advice. At the age of five, I started pre-school where I learned how to count and to say my ABC's. This was an odd sort of paradoxical situation, especially since I'd learned how to burglarize a house a year earlier.

My mom was a hard-working woman trying to make ends meet while raising three kids on her own. Times were tough and she needed help; like a knight in shining armor riding a snow white horse, my future stepfather rode into our lives in a pale yellow Mercury Marquis. From the beginning, I was terrorized with beatings. Some of them occurred while I was bound and gagged. Tied to a banister of a stairwell or a headpost of the bed, I was often beaten unconscious. My mother's knight became our personal torturer.

The beatings got worse. As a junior high student, I would often go to school with knots on my head, eye sockets as big as baseballs and once, even a broken leg. When asked what happened, I would recite the usual, "I got stung by bees," or "I fell." My teachers had begun to recognize the pattern of abuse, but no one intervened. There was no one to talk to; if I talked, I would have to pay the piper later.

To escape the pain, I would run away from home in search of my biological father. Surely he would help me and make the beatings stop? What occurred probably became the turning point in my life. Rather than getting the help I so desperately needed from my true father, I got returned home to my stepfather who couldn't wait to get his hands on me. Some nights I would wake up and my stepfather would have guns pointed at my head. I would scream and beg for him not to kill me. The neighbors knew what was happening. The schools knew what was happening. The police officers dispatched to our house when he beat me and my mother knew what was happening. So why was this allowed to continue?

I grew angry with the world and started shop-lifting, skipping school and gang fighting. Now I was in control. I was the one with a gun; guns gave me power, I rationalized, and I wanted empowerment. But my guns and empowerment only got me hospitalized for wounds sustained in shootouts.

In the mid-eighties, I'd been through several transitions, including getting a GED and going to a business college, even squaring up and having kids. I worked for the Board of Education as a custodian for several years, but I started getting disillusioned and turned back to the street life. Everything that I had seen earlier in my life I had slowly but surely become. I started trafficking drugs from Miami to Atlanta. I often kept company with pimps and exotic dancers. Mr. James Edward Camp Jr. was my closest friend and beloved adviser during those times. If it were not for him, I surely would have perished long ago, but the lessons I learned from him still could not keep me from an inevitable fate -- prison.

In the street life, nothing is sure, not your life, not your money or your precious cars and jewelry. One day you've got it and the next day it can all fade into oblivion. So everyday becomes the proverbial, never-ending "paperchase." You begin to worship money and you'll do anything to get it.

On one of my paperchases, I walked into a pawnshop owned by someone whom I had known very well, a person who had always been very kind to me, and I robbed him. I was arrested a few months later and quickly made bond. My mind was still focused on hustling, no matter what the consequences were. So a few days after I was released on bond for the armed robbery, I took a flight to Miami to buy cocaine. The seriousness of the robbery was insignificant to my need to support my grand lifestyle. I returned to Atlanta and began dealing again.

Then, in a strange twist of fate, I was robbed -- not by the usual suspects, the everyday, hanging-on-the-corner hoodlum. I was robbed by three of Atlanta's finest, police officers of the drug task force called the "Red Dogs." This police unit spread their reign of terror throughout Atlanta's primarily black communities, virtually waging war and holding whole neighborhoods under siege. Charges of corruption and police brutality against the officers were always dismissed and their actions ruled justified, even in the most extreme cases where drug suspects died in police custody.

On Feb. 8, 1991, I also became a statistic, just another beating victim who would be swept under the rug, silenced by being hidden away in the judicial system. That evening I was kidnapped and, well after midnight, I was savagely beaten and tortured. I was kicked in the face until I was unrecognizable, then beaten repeatedly from head to toe with a very large metal flashlight and night stick. Pistol to my head, bound in handcuffs and gagged with my own sock to muffle my horrific screams for help, I started to pray for the first time in my entire life. I too almost died in police custody, merely a statistic.

The officers were fired amid extensive media coverage. I was shipped off to prison from the county jail without being convicted of any crime, and hidden there until news reporters tracked me down. Death threats were made on my life and a key witness against the officers was found dead behind an apartment building, stabbed several times. The Grand Jury refused to indict the officers, and the city's Civilian Review Panel made the recommendation to reinstate them -- business as usual for all parties involved, except for the naive key player who went to court for the armed robbery and received a life plus 25 year sentence.

While the drama was unfolding and I was all alone in my assigned cell in the lock-down unit of Coastal State Prison, I found more than a few moments to reflect on my stormy childhood. I could visualize many of my life's little ironies; many of the things that I've gone through as a child re-surfaced. The cycle of pain had come full circle. Strange things happen in the mind when a person is confined. Thoughts become like thunder in the solitude and the silence. That's when realization takes hold and the awakening is enough to "shake the conscience." I felt like the fabled character Rip Van Winkle! I'd been asleep for over two decades. Of course I was overwhelmed with feelings of confusion, anger and finally guilt. Suddenly I realized I didn't even know who I was. It would seem I'd spent my entire life running away from responsibilities and pain and in "looking for love in all the wrong places." Rather than give up,

I learned a lot about myself. I found an inner strength and began to develop a new self-image. I was starting over, despite the fact that I was sitting in a cell, isolated from the rest of the world. A simple adjustment in thinking and I was on my way to changing. It was the first right decision I'd made in a long time.

I have been in prison for nine years. From the beginning, I knew the odds were stacked against me, especially with a sentence that is considered the equivalent of "walking dead." My first couple of years in prison were served in high security camps: Coastal, Dodge, Hancock and Smith, Hancock and Smith being "gladiator" schools. At any moment without provocation, gang fighting would erupt -- Atlanta vs. Augusta, GA; Atlanta vs. Albany, GA; Atlanta vs. Savannah, GA, etc. Being the state's capitol, Atlanta alone was enough to fuel petty jealousies and envy that would cause armed battles. Because most of Atlanta's adversaries were from smaller towns and rural communities, they would often be outnumbered. So an alliance was formed among them, creating the "Down South Hustlers." Of course there were other bangers -- Crips, Bloods and the fastest growing of these units, the Folks Gang. But they were new and didn't have the allure of the established gangs of "The City," Atlanta's P's and G's (pimps and gangsters), and South Georgia's Down South Hustlers.

It was November of 1992 when I arrived at Hancock. It was noticeably different from any prison I'd served time in before. It was huge, with masses of razorwire that could be seen for miles. After exiting the transfer bus and being processed, I walked out of the ID section into a mob of old friends -- people I knew from the streets and prisoners I'd known in other prisons. On the inside, we just referred to each other as "home boys." They had known of my arrival days before I'd left my last prison and were there to welcome me at the fence that holds them in a secured area. I was unofficially dubbed a leader because of the many fights I'd won and because of my reputation for "handling my business" on the streets. This was the mark of a real man, the ghetto testament to true manhood, plus I had charisma. In my world it meant instant popularity.

I was temporarily assigned to a transient cell block. The two tier block holds 96 men, most of whom are lifers and have very little to look forward to. This was it, the end of the line. The things that now gave my life substance were contained in a 3 x 2 box. I entered the cell block carrying everything I owned. Everyone froze in silence as all of the new arrivals stopped at the control center. The officer on duty handed us our cell assignments and said, "Welcome to Hell." Then, as if by command, came whispers and an orchestrated chorus of loud roars: "Fresh meat! Fresh meat!" Some of the men who had arrived with me were white males no more than 19, first time in, not a good combination in a predatory environment. Before the lights had gone out that night, and while I was rapping with my homies, the young white boys were being raped.

I was a gang leader and highly respected by inmates and the administration alike. I was "Spoon," a player from The City who exemplified cunning and wit. I was untouchable in fights and riots. Growing up in the streets had taught me the "rules of conduct" that define what is proper and improper for whom and under what conditions. So in certain instances, I had an edge; I was the stereotypical TV convict and I was smart.

Despite many of the ridiculously over-simplified stereotypes about prison life, drugs really are rampant and can produce a lot of cash. The proceeds from the drug money are used to buy favors from the usually under-paid, under-educated guards, so the money becomes power and the one who possesses the power inevitably runs the prison. Virtually anything becomes possible: sexual favors from female guards and staff, escape tools, guns and knives, assassinations (hits) and, of course, more and more drugs.

The subculture of the streets was alive and thriving. "Prison isn't any different from the ghetto," I thought. It was all just a matter of survival of the fittest, and only the strong survive. With certain elements firmly intact, the competition for control over the drug trade turned bloody. In January of 1993 through the summer of 1994, gang violence escalated to previously unseen proportions all over the state. Hancock was not immune. Administrators were powerless to control the armed confrontations between gang rivals.

During one of the City skirmishes with the Down South Hustlers, I was stabbed in the face and had to be transported immediately to a hospital outside of the prison. While I was lying there on the examination table being attended to by the nurse, the doctor entered the room. As he worked to stop the bleeding, he talked to me about the senseless violence going on down at the prison. He was a doctor at the Sparta Medical Center and he had seen his share of casualties of war. He directed my attention to the adjacent room. There was another patient there from the prison, but he wasn't as lucky as I was. I was just stabbed in the face. The patient across the hall was being treated for massive head trauma and heart failure; he was dying. The life expectancy for black males is 25, but for gang members the numbers are considerably lower, maybe 18 or 19. Most gang members never reach prison, because they die on the streets. If they do make it to prison, they're lucky, incredibly skilled or both. This is the ugly paradox.

After my stay at the hospital, I was returned to the prison and escorted directly to the lock-down unit. My life was in shambles. I felt like just giving up. Until then, I had been content to serve my time with my homies, fighting and getting high or whatever the gang lifestyle dictated, but my mind wasn't satisfied and I started to regret what I had done. I felt a hungering inside of me that I didn't know how to satisfy. I had allowed myself to get pulled into the very things I wanted to avoid. I had broken the promises I'd made to my friends and family, and most of all, I'd broken the promises I'd made to myself a few years earlier while in the lockdown unit at Coastal. I wasn't smart anymore -- I quickly realized I was really dumb!

I had already experienced more than my share of disappointments and I refused to accept the idea that prison would be my last stop. I could not end my life as a failure, so I allowed my mind to expand and willed my soul to survive the court-appointed living death. At first, I got laughed at for participating in the self-help programs that were available through counseling.

After all, I am a lifer. In Georgia, this usually means that you are more likely to die in prison than to be released. I did not let this sway me and continued to participate in the counseling groups.

Most of the self-help programs concentrated on deterring "criminal thinking" and "behavioral problems." Because they are learned behaviors, they can be modified and made to be less extreme through therapy. The primary rule of participation is admitting that there is a problem. If and when this is accomplished, the process of healing can begin. Quite naturally, prisoners have a constant preoccupation with "getting out." Though getting out is an honest goal, it cannot be the sole motivation for entering therapy sessions. The truth of the matter is that some prisoners have an unsubstantiated belief that group participation will automatically qualify them for parole. This is totally wrong! Entering group therapy sessions should be a rewarding experience for those who are truly in search of the place to begin the tedious process of correcting the afflictions within. The process should not be diminished or belittled by individuals with ulterior motives. There are those group participants who realize that they possess serious anti-social behaviors that are contrary to the welfare of society. These are the participants who display the most sincere willingness to address their real behavioral problems and thinking errors.

If you can somehow inspire an incarcerated person, whether through sports, counseling, vocational tech or general education classes, you can inevitably alter the thinking processes of this individual. This principle was never more evident than when I participated as a facilitator in a substance abuse treatment program at Smith State Prison. I'd never worked as a counselor and the experience was exciting, to say the least. I was really surprised at my group's willingness to participate. Usually prisoners are reluctant to open up in group settings; this has been my personal observation in the numerous self-help programs in which I've participated. Those groups were primarily led by a prison's staff counselor; because of this the men were hesitant to share their experiences. Staff members are always seen as outsiders. Therefore, certain information is never revealed for fear of becoming a detriment at a later date, mainly in a parole eligibility consideration hearing.

The Substance Abuse Treatment Program (SATP), now that was something innovative -- a peer group facilitated by an inmate counselor. It was a diverse group which consisted of drug and alcohol abusers, sexual offenders and batterers of women. There were men of different age groups, racial, social and economic backgrounds. One of the main topics of discussion was substance abuse and understanding that addiction has serious medical and social consequences.

The National Institute of Alcohol Abuse and Alcoholism and the National Institute on Drug Abuse estimated in a recently released study that the economic cost of alcohol and drug abuse was $246 billion in 1992, the most recent year for which sufficient data was available. This study confirms the enormous damage done to society by alcohol related and drug related problems. Many of the participants in SATP admitted to drug and alcohol use prior to committing criminal acts. In my opinion, rather than incarcerating people with addictions, law makers should allocate a larger portion of the huge criminal justice expenditures towards drug abuse intervention and rehabilitative programs. This would be the most effective area to focus on. Realistically speaking, if it were not for alcohol and drug use, most incarcerated individuals would not be there.

In my group's first meeting, the atmosphere was thick. I could feel the tension and disbelief of having a peer in a leadership role, especially in a group where confidentiality was a priority. I began the meeting by introducing myself, describing the program, the objectives and their requirements as participants. The presentation was formal and, to my surprise, no one questioned my ability to lead the group. Over the 30-day intensive therapy, I witnessed men talk about their fears, their hopes and dreams for a better life -- a life free of whatever ills may have plagued them on the streets and brought them to prison. In them I saw bits and pieces of my own life's experiences. It was at that time that I realized it is safe to admit my powerlessness and just be human. I also learned that being humble does not mean being weak. It means accepting ourselves and our strengths as well as our weaknesses.

As a rule, most of us have serious problems with admitting our mistakes and admitting when we are wrong; we set unrealistic standards for ourselves. It's at these times we need to take a good look at ourselves and ask the question, "What makes me so much better than him?" When one group of people is seen as perfect and the other as worthless, it creates a subclass. Furthermore, when this happens, the class of people that are seen as worthless are dehumanized beyond barbarism. This type of dehumanization is occurring on a massive scale here in the United States, with Georgia being the eighth leading incarcerator of her people.

Since the passage of the "two strikes and you're out" law by the Georgia Legislature and its well-known counterpart, the 90% policy adopted by the Parole Board, Georgia's county jails and prisons have filled to capacity and overflowed. At Dooly State Prison, every square inch is accounted for. It's so overcrowded that the administration has begun to manufacture bunks which elevate three-men high, the first bunk being only six inches from the floor. Space designated for a single man now holds three. Georgia's prison population has more than doubled from 18,000 in 1989 to 40,000 in 1998, the state spending $700 million a year on its corrections system. The Georgia Board of Pardons and Paroles said that by 2003, the state will have just 42,000 prison beds for a projected 55,000 state prisoners.

This imbalance is primarily due to the "two strikes" law, inconsistencies in sentencing, and parole board policies requiring felons convicted of any of 20 specific crimes to serve at least 90% of their sentences. There is evidence that parolees are a small segment of Georgia's criminal justice population, one which has a minimal impact on new crime. Georgia law and tough parole policies guarantee that persons convicted of violent crimes will serve long, hard prison sentences. Yet crime still occurs, new victims suffer and the state needs more prison beds. Tough sentencing may remove a few criminals from the streets, but what these laws don't do is deter the thousands of new criminals who quickly replace them.

Every election year, prisoners bear an extra burden. Politicians in their arrogance and avarice forget that the people they so coldly use as pawns are living, breathing, thinking human beings. The candidates would have the general public believe that prisons are places with too many luxuries and that rehabilitation isn't an attainable goal. With this idea, I vehemently disagree!

I've seen and experienced firsthand the corrective powers of self-help programs, vocational training and the general education of incarcerated persons. So why have education and job training been targeted as expendable, especially when it has been documented that these programs reduce the recidivism rate of parolees? It seems they have fallen prey to political prostitution. In 1997, 927 parolees were returned to prison. The way the system is structured today, it is almost a certainty that parolees in the state of Georgia will reoffend within a year of their release. This is simply because of their prolonged suffering while in prison, and a systematic daily regime that is designed to instill into them resentment and hatred toward authority figures. These men are essentially leaving prison naked and returning to a world that puts an emphasis on fine clothing.

To be absolutely frank, parolees aren't being given the right motivation to succeed, nor are they being given the right rehabilitative tools while in prison to effect a successful transition into society. It is time for the citizens of this country to take an interest in seeing that their tax dollars are used in a manner which is consistent with true public agenda, not media and political hype.

Georgia, unlike many states that pay inmates for their labor, releases a parolee back into society with a grand total of $35; $10 of this was deducted from any funds the prisoner may have obtained from family or friends during his incarceration. So actually the state of Georgia only contributes $25 toward a newly released prisoner's return to society; no other assistance is provided.

There are incarceration alternatives that allow prisoners a slower reintegration into society. Halfway houses and transitional centers are viable options and a realistic means of returning prisoners back into their communities. It is extremely unlikely that long-term violent offenders will qualify, which doesn't make sense and is inconsistent with statistics that rate long-term prisoners as those most likely to successfully make the transition. Halfway houses are strictly run links between prison and society; they are places where prisoners are allowed to seek gainful employment under the watchful eye of staff. The benefits of a supervised release of the prisoner outweighs the risks of releasing an inmate into the community unsupervised. This method of reintegration has been proven to reduce the chance of a prisoner's return to lock up.

I strongly believe that success is forthcoming for myself and for others that have made errors in judgment, but refuse to succumb to psychological and social stigmas placed upon them. The political rhetoric of the '90s is quickly becoming played out. Voters and people directly involved with law enforcement and corrections see firsthand the chaos created by the "get tough on crime" campaign. Politicians are no longer able to sell the informed citizens fried ice cream. Dirty politics and negative commercials only validate suspicions of corruption in public office, leaving voters with the unpleasantness of choosing the lesser of two evils. Meanwhile, more and more freedoms guaranteed under the Constitution are being eroded.

The question is asked, "What do newly released prisoners need to aid them in making a successful transition into society?" The answer varies; each case has to be evaluated and handled on an individual basis. No two prisoners are the same, even if their lifestyles and crimes were similar. This is why a better system of assessing prisoners' needs while in prison, and especially upon release, is imperative. There should be a community-based organization which takes these assessments and offers genuine assistance. Job referrals, temporary housing, drug and alcohol counseling, food and clothing vouchers, access to mass transit -- these are the real needs of a released prisoner. Instead, our current corrections' policies do nothing to intervene in, and may actually help to perpetuate, the cycle of crime.

The single parent matriarchy exists in disproportionate numbers in the black communities. Black women are often left with the responsibility of trying to raise a male child and performing the dual role of mother and father. This is primarily due to father abandonment and increased incarceration rates of black males in the United States. It is a growing phenomena that has a direct correlation to the problems that children of prisoners face, such as delinquency, poor performance in school, suicide, drug addiction and alcoholism. The male children of prisoners are more at risk than their female siblings or white counterparts.

I have three teenage boys from three different relationships. Communication hasn't been easy for me because of the complexities associated with each of their individual family lives. Willie Jr. and Demonte still reside in the Atlanta area, but Jamal and his mother are no longer living in Georgia. Parenting from behind bars is seemingly impossible. For success, both parents must maintain a healthy line of communication. When there is resentment and anger between the parents, they must be set aside for the children's sake. Understanding this situation and being a father incapacitated by incarceration, I've had to continually redefine the art of parenting. Similarly, I've had to undergo a series of growth changes within myself before I could fully grasp the magnitude of the responsibilities I hold toward my children. I didn't want my boys to inherit a legacy of shame and continue to perpetuate the vicious cycle of crime. I wanted to be an active participant in their lives, but how?

The only means of communication available was visits, letters and phone calls. Many times visits were impossible because of the great distances and for economic reasons. Phone calls are extremely costly and presented an extra financial burden to the mothers. So I opted to write letters as much as possible. When I wrote, I expressed my love and I tried to convey to them the importance of an education and the dangers of anti-social behaviors. Even before they were able to read, I would send them greeting cards for their mothers to read to them. Whenever possible, I would divert funds sent to me by friends to my sons. It wasn't much, but the gesture did more to bridge the gap than I had anticipated. There were times, many times, I went without so that I would be able to perform this act. But isn't that what parenting is all about, sacrifice?

If physical contact and financial support are impossible, prisoners must become active participants in their children's emotional lives. There is no one formula for parenting behind bars. Each and every one of us who have children must follow our hearts and discover new ways to cross the physical barriers of prison. In many instances, our children are all we have accomplished in our lives that are inherently good. It's easy for absent fathers to say that they love their children; love is the easy part. It's turning the love into loving that makes the real difference to the child. When your children respect you and voluntarily do what is expected of them, this is your reward.

It is my greatest fear to wake up one day and see one of my sons walking into prison. I've cried and prayed many nights that God will protect them and keep them from suffering the same fate as mine. They too, like myself, have not had the benefit of being reared by both natural parents, which increases their risk of continuing the cycle. It is a circle that must be broken here, now and forever, and I guess it all begins with me -- their father.

The United States must also display the courage and accept the responsibilities of parenting a growing nation. If your child broke a rule, would you lock her in a cage or a basement and throw away the key? Of course not! You would talk to that child. You would teach that child right from wrong. Even if this child continued to break rules, you, as a parent, would not simply hide that child away in a dark closet as a means of dealing with the problem. But America is hiding its children in jails and prisons across the nation. It's time Americans dealt with their issues in a manner which is truly reflective of our progressive society and a changing world. Stop sweeping prisoners under the rug. Help us to change. Help others as you have helped me -- to undergo a metamorphosis.

"Since that first morning when I crawled into the world, a naked grubby thing, and found the world unkind, my dearest faith has been that this is but a trial: I shall be changed." Hornworm: Autumn Lamentation by Stanley Kunitz

Willie Christopher Tucker is currently working toward his degree in Developmental Psychology through Ohio University's Independent Study Program. He has been incarcerated for over nine years, during which time he has worked as a substance abuse counselor. He is also working on his certification in the use of Microsoft Office Suite applications software at Wheeler Correctional Facility where he is presently incarcerated. He is a member of the American Civil Liberties Union and the National Coalition to Abolish the Death Penalty. Willie is the poetry editor and feature poet for the Internet prisoner magazine, CellDoor. His poetry has appeared in Trapped Under Ice: A Death Row Anthology (1995), Frontiers of Justice, Volume 2: Coddling or Common Sense? (1998), and the magazine Quaker Life. Willie is from Atlanta, Georgia's Poolecreek. He was expelled from Walter George High School and told by school officials that he would never amount to anything. He believes that there is the capacity to change within everyone and that no one should be told that he is insignificant, especially not a child. His hope for the future is to become an advocate for juvenile offenders and children with AIDS.

FACING MYSELF

Paul Everson

My name is Paul Everson. Over the Labor Day weekend of 1982, I took the life of a prominent University of Florida professor. In the summer of 1983, I was sentenced to life with a mandatory-minimum 25 years before eligibility for parole. I had recently turned 18 when I committed the crime.

It's hard for me to explain just what led me to commit murder. I don't know. It's not an act I ever gave thought to or wondered about. I never questioned whether or not I was capable of it. It just happened. The victim owed one of my friends money for sexual favors and he refused to pay, so we stole one of his checks and got busted trying to cash it. Once in jail, I learned that one of the others was a juvenile. We used this information against him and he dropped the charges against us. One of us had a chat with him as charges were being dropped, and he said he would pay what he owed and that the money would be left in the mailbox. When we got there, he was gone and there was no money. Rather than count our losses and leave, we waited for him to come home.

We waited for three days, but during that time the topic of murdering him never came up. Although there was some anger towards him for sending me and my co-defendants to jail on the forgery charge, I don't believe that anger was the motivation. I wasn't consciously angry. When he finally came home, we approached him about the money and once again he refused to pay. That's when things got out of hand and in the end he was asphyxiated. I participated in his death, but he didn't owe the money to me. I should have stayed out of it, but for some reason I didn't. I could probably list fifty reasons why I participated -- peer pressure, loyalty towards friends, the rise of suppressed anger towards my father? It could have been any one of them or a combination of all of them. The point is that I don't know. During my years of incarceration, I have never asked myself why I did it. I think part of me might fear the answer.

It's been said that some/most murderers come from broken homes. That may be true in some cases, but not in mine. The relationship between me and my father was never anything to be proud of, but don't confuse our relationship with my home life. My home life was good. Neither parent abused drugs or alcohol, there was always food on the table, a nice house, safe schools and a stable community where the crime rate was low. What started the whole thing was something my father once said to me, and he picked the wrong age to say it. My father and I never bonded and that's the core of the problem. Children form a bond with their parents at a very early age and that bond teaches children how to love and care. In order for the child to become whole, there has to be a bond between the child and both parents. That didn't happen in my case. When I was around five years old, my father sat me down on my bed and told me that as a son he had to love me, but as a person he would always hate my guts. What a five year old child could do to deserve to hear those words is a mystery to me.

Those words stuck with me. It would have been different if he had apologized for saying them, but he didn't. He just got up and left me sitting there crying. I never looked at my father the same way after that, convinced that my father hated me, so I taught myself to hate him. My mother never knew what he had said to me.

I started rebelling after that. I wanted him to feel the hurt I carried in knowing he hated me, so I went out of my way to hurt him. The emotional damage I inflicted made me feel better, but eventually the hate I held towards him began to swallow me. It got to the point where I needed to be around miserable people. I fed off of it like a psychic vampire. The misery, depression, sorrow and pain that flowed from people made me feel alive. If there was no misery around, then I would create some. My mom would ask me why I did it. My therapists would ask me why I did it. I could never give them an answer because I wasn't consciously aware of why I was doing it. My awareness now is only through my reflection back on things.

Back then I had no conception of mental abuse. Any time I heard of abuse, it was either sexual or physical, which is why I used to say I did not come from an abusive family. I don't say that now. Several years back, I read a book called The Kids Next Door. It was about kids who have killed one or both parents for whatever reason. It was in this book I learned about mental abuse.

Coming out of the closet only made things worse, but I think I did it to hurt him. I didn't just wake up one day and tell him I was gay. I woke up one day wondering how to tell both my parents. I was 14 at the time. I went to a crisis center and met with a woman named Marilyn. I asked her how I could tell my parents I was gay with minimal damage, mostly for my mother. I knew my father would go nuts, but my hatred towards him was more than nine years old by this time and I didn't really care what it did to him. However, I didn't want to hurt my mother because by this time she and I had bonded and I knew she loved me. I've never had to question it and at times it bothered me to know that my hatred towards my father was catching her in the crossfire.

Marilyn counseled me twice a week for almost a year. One day, when she knew that I was comfortable inside with my sexuality, she made a telephone call. My mother came up and she and Marilyn talked. I sat in the waiting room for 15 or 20 minutes, although it seemed like forever. They came out of the office and my mom asked me if I was ready to go. She seemed fine. Maybe it was denial, but she seemed okay with it. She said, "I suspected." When I asked what made her suspicious, she said, "I'm your mother. Mothers know." We went shopping and on the way home, I asked her not to tell my father. I told her I would tell him when I was ready.

We got home and I brought the last bag of groceries into the house. I was met at the door by my father saying, "So you're queer, huh?" His words had the impact of a two by four across the face. I looked at my mother to let her know I felt betrayed and she said, "He's my husband. I had to tell him." My father responded with, "Hey, don't worry about it. Some families raise doctors and some families raise lawyers. Me, I raise queers." It was a reaction I had expected, but all it did was compound what I already felt towards him.

I made the choice to tell them because I had to. See, "coming out" isn't just telling the world you're gay. Coming out is honesty. It's honesty towards yourself. It's admitting it to yourself, and if you can't be honest to yourself, you damn sure can't be honest with anyone else. Sometimes coming out can be a wonderful thing and sometimes it can be the biggest mistake you've ever made. For me it was both. It was wonderful because I didn't have to hide it anymore, but it was a mistake because people weren't as understanding as I had thought they would be.

My bitterness and/or anger wasn't the reason my school stepped in. That was caused by my refusal to pay attention to the teacher. It wasn't a question of my abilities. I was quite able; I once got all A's and B's on my report card, just to prove I could do it. The problem was I didn't want to do it and no one was going to make me. I refused to do homework. I refused to do most classroom assignments. I did manage to pass most of my tests, though. I read the books. I didn't need a teacher; I opened the book in class and read it. What the teacher was saying was pointless because I was past it. While the teacher was talking about the sixteenth century, I was already reading about the seventeenth.

I was flagged for special education in the sixth grade. They thought I had A.D.D. and figured a smaller class with fewer students would make it easier for me to pay attention. After a couple of months, they realized it was useless and they put me back in regular classes. The same school went out of its way to allow me entry into their kitchen. I don't remember exactly why they decided to do it, but after school I was allowed to work with the baker. As far as I know, I was the only one. It lasted the school year and I really enjoyed it. It didn't change anything, though. Come the end of the school year, I was the same old bitter kid. I don't really know what the goal of the program was; I never questioned why they let me do it and they never volunteered the information.

My parents repeatedly sent me to counseling, but all the counselors found me to be a normal kid; they couldn't find anything "wrong" with me. Even though the counseling and the special activities were designed to help me, they didn't prevent anything. If there is a "Crime Zone," I was in it. Mostly what brought me into it was me, nothing more. When I wanted something, I took it. I owed nothing to life, but life owed everything to me and I was going to collect. I was big on stealing cars. If I saw a car I wanted, I would steal it, drive around for a couple of days, run out of gas, ditch it and steal another one. Eventually, I got caught and was sent to a juvenile detention center for six months. While I was there, I never gave thought as to what they might be able to do to help me. My perception was there was nothing wrong with me, which meant there was nothing to change.

I don't remember much about the juvenile center I was in. I was there for six months, but I don't recall any programs. I don't even recall having to go to school while I was there. I remember only two counselors and my room, but I know I was treated well. I particularly remember one counselor, a man I'll keep nameless, because when I ran away at 16 and got involved with prostitution, he picked me up as a "client." He remembered me, but my stay at the juvenile center never came up.

What led me into prostitution was circumstance. I could have gone home, but the friction between me and my father prevented me from doing that. It was to the point where we couldn't spend five minutes in the same room. There was nothing specific that set him off; all it took was my presence. If there were people around he was fine, but when we were alone I was a nothing, I would never amount to anything. Having a "queer" kid was an embarrassment to him. He once told me that if he had thought for one minute one of his kids would be "queer," he would have made my mother have an abortion. Aside from my mother, I was never close to anyone in my family. I have two brothers, one older, one younger, but we've never seen eye-to-eye. As for grandparents, aunts, uncles, cousins, etc., forget it. Ours was never a close-knit family. Usually we would all get together on Thanksgiving and Christmas and every year we'd all regret it.

At 16, I had just had enough and I left home for good. No goodbye, no notes, I just left. We were living on Cape Cod at the time; I had a little money, so I bought a bus ticket to Boston. I got off the bus and when I left the terminal, a car pulled up. A man told me how much he would give me and what for. I agreed and that's what started it.

I don't know if self-esteem plays any role in being a whore. I don't really recall how I felt about myself -- I was too busy hating my father to notice. But regardless of how I felt the first time I sold myself, when the night ended and I had made over one thousand dollars, I felt pretty good. It was a rush of a whole different kind. I rented a hotel room and after a shower and a few hours sleep, I went shopping. I bought all new clothes; that night I got all spiffed up and went out again. I turned only one trick that night. One twelve-hundred dollar trick. I was euphoric. Not only was I making money, I was making it by doing something I enjoyed doing. I worked the streets of Boston for about a year before I decided to go to New York.

New York was so different. The city was brighter, faster, more energetic. Whatever high I got from Boston, New York intensified it. Hustling the streets of New York is a challenge. It's fast paced, quick money and it's so easy to get caught up in. I hit New York when I was 17 years old. I was very good looking and I used those looks to get anything and everything I wanted. It's simple economics -- supply and demand.

86

Prostitution is an addiction. It gets into your veins and it stays there. It can also be dangerous. I was fortunate enough not to have had anything bad happen to me, but I've had friends who were raped, severely beaten, even murdered. It's an underground world all its own, the likes of which you've never seen before, but I can honestly say that if I thought for one minute I could do it again, I would.

Don't misunderstand. I'm not glorifying prostitution. I don't recommend teenagers leave home and become whores. If I knew someone who was contemplating it, I would do my best to try and talk him out of it. But for me personally, it gave me a chance to make a lot of money, to meet interesting people and to visit a lot of interesting places. In essence, I learned how to carry myself in a more sophisticated, educated manner. I've been to swank parties as the nephew of a millionaire and I've been in a sleazy motel room dressed as an altar boy.

Like I said, it's a drug. You set a limit of how much you'll make one night. You get all dressed up and you go out. You make your quota and you go home. Sounds easy, right? Trust me, it's not, because while you're sitting in your apartment or motel/hotel room, you can hear the streets calling you. It says, "There's more where that came from." Before you know it, you're back out there selling your ass to the highest bidder.

Some whores end up junkies. I guess I'm lucky I wasn't one of them, but I've worked with plenty who were and it wasn't pretty. Even though it was glorious, for lack of a better word, for me, I don't recommend it for anyone. It's not a life to live. Actually it's not a life at all. It's a mere existence. It's lonely. You have to maintain a professional detachment. You can't care for anyone, and after being like that for a prolonged period of time, you become hardened and cold inside.

Some whores have pimps. Pimps are bad news and it's wise to avoid them if you can, but sometimes you can't. Back in my day, it was common for someone to come up and say, "Billy B. says he'll swing by at midnight. If you don't have $500 for him, you're in trouble." Sure enough, at midnight one of Billy B.'s thugs would show up and if you didn't hand him the money, you would get the shit beat out of you but good. That's all it takes. You've been tagged and you now work for Billy B.

Most gay male whores look for "sugardaddies." A sugardaddy is a pipe dream and most don't find one. You have to have some irresistible qualities that most just don't possess. Find one and you're all set, right? Wrong. You're a commodity. You come a dime a dozen and usually better can be found. Most sugardaddies are perverts, aka "chicken hawks," preying off young kids. They pass you around at parties and you have sex with all their friends. They dress you up in fancy clothes and take pictures of you. Want to know where those pictures go? They go to other chicken hawks. And when "daddy" wants to make home movies of you and another kid from the "stable" getting it on, or he wants to take dirty pictures of you, where do you think those movies or dirty pictures go? That's right -- other chicken hawks. Please don't think for one minute those items are given away as tokens of friendship. They're not. They're sold for hundreds or even thousands of dollars. At the risk of repeating myself, you're a commodity.

More often than not, once you find a sugardaddy, you've hit a dead end street. If you try to leave before they're through with you, they'll spend hours brainwashing you into believing you can't make it without them. They'll convince you no one will want you; in most cases, you end up staying. In the event you do leave, you'll never have another client again. Word will spread throughout the "community" that you're trouble, i.e. you rob clients, or you're really straight and you "bash" gay old men, or any number of false statements. Believe me, I've heard some good ones and it works.

The other side of the coin is just as bad. After daddy earns your complete and utter trust, he'll take you on a trip, usually somewhere "quiet," "out of the way." Daddy will find some reason to have to go out for a while, but don't worry -- he'll be back for you. No, he won't. You're stuck there. Good luck finding your way back, because I'm willing to bet you weren't paying attention to how you got there in the first place. You can take a cab or a bus, right? Wrong. Daddy will make sure you have no money. Cops? No, being stranded is simply an occupational hazard. Besides, you'd never even think of going to the cops; the thought would never enter your mind. When you do finally get back, your name will be mud and you'll find no work. Another way they get rid of you is you go out one night and when you come home, the doorman won't let you in, or you get in and all the locks have been changed. You call and the phone's been disconnected. None of it was in your name, so you're back on the streets and your name is shit. You walk the streets all night begging for a twenty dollar trick; when dawn breaks, you're still out there with nothing. You end up sleeping in the subway, provided you have the fifty cents for a token to get in.

Either way it goes, sugardaddies will get rid of you and ruin you when they're finished with you. If that doesn't happen, you'll face burn out. Clients will just get tired of seeing your mug on the block and they'll ignore you as they drive by. Burn out equals early retirement with no pension. You'll end up in the gutter unless you were smart enough to save some of that money you made. Fortunately, I never went through any of what I just relayed to you, but I know many who have.

See, I was smart. If you want to be a successful whore, you have to know how to manipulate. For lack of a better phrase, I sub-contracted my services. My chicken hawk didn't find me, I found him. I was selective in the process. I asked questions and when I found the right one, I poured on the charm. The trick was to convince him he needed me when in all actuality he didn't. My hawk liked taking pictures and making movies and he was open about it. He was a prominent businessman who worked in Manhattan but lived in New Jersey with his wife and daughter. He couldn't afford to be seen driving around the streets of New York picking up kids. In time, I became a "stable boy," a scout of sorts. It was my job to locate runaway kids, boys or girls, usually 14, 15, 16 years old. I would bring them "home" and they would be wined, dined and spoiled. Then came the pictures and the home movies and after a couple of weeks, the kid/kids was/were gone and I received a "finder's fee." I don't know what happened to them after they left. I never saw them again and at that time I didn't care. When they were gone, I would go scout more. This kept me off the streets for long periods of time, so I never faced burnout and I supplemented my income at the same time. In all actuality, it was white slavery. I'm not proud of that now. If I hadn't come to prison, there's no telling where I'd be today. My guess is dead.

My life was a roller coaster which was out of control. The only way it was going to stop was to crash. And it did. I honestly believed I would be the one who ended up dead; I never imagined I would end up killing someone.

Prison is probably the biggest life-altering event you could ever experience -- if you survive it. A lot don't. Being in prison takes a strong mind and some just don't have it and choose suicide as a way out. Sadly, prison has a way of taking as many lives as it may save, but with all its negativity and violence, prison can be a positive experience if you let it. You have to want it though. Rehabilitation is not something which can be forced upon a person. There has to be an inner desire to change, otherwise all attempts will fail. Prison can afford an opportunity for a person to take a step back and look at his/her life. I did that and I didn't like what I saw, so I started the change. It was one of the hardest things I've ever had to do.

Prison in and of itself is a very negative place. That negativity runs deep throughout staff as well as inmates. Most guards are miserable people leading miserable lives to begin with; from experience, miserable people enjoy being in miserable places. Many guards have a psychological need for control and this is the opportune environment to feed that need. But states are desperate for people to work their prisons and jails, and most states don't question mental status. By the same token, there are guards who are just in it for a paycheck. They don't care what happens as long as they don't see it. If they see it, they have to act on it and they don't want to do that. They just do their eight hours and leave.

Prison is not very different from society, not as different as some think. Prison can best be described as a city within a city. This city has its own social structure, its own economical structure, its own political structure, its own religious structure and its own laws and codes. Some cell blocks are dirty, complete dives, while others are well kept, clean. Most of the clean areas are known as "honor" dorms or "privileged" living areas. You have to remain free from disciplinary infractions to be placed there and continue living there. Some jobs don't pay or don't pay well and some do. You have to start at the bottom and work your way up, as you would in society. You work your way into a better living area and you work your way into the higher paying jobs. Granted, we don't have physical freedom, but we live freely within the bounds of our environment. In a nutshell, life continues.

As with society, there are any number of ways of making yourself a better person while you're here. Most prisons offer college classes through local universities. Contrary to popular belief, they are not free; we do have to pay for them. There was a time when prisoners were eligible to receive Pell Grants for college, but even though prisoners made up less than one percent of people receiving Pell Grants, they were taken away from us.

There are a number of therapists working in prisons. Whether they are social workers, psychologists, psychiatrists or any combination thereof, they are here for you. The prisons I have been to have all offered courses in anger management, aggression management and Journey to Self classes. I was fortunate enough to have had the opportunity to take a Dianetics course. Facing myself was the hardest thing I've ever done. Once I began seeing myself, I realized I had to change. I didn't have a role model or a hero to model myself after. I just wanted to be different than I was. I wanted to like myself. I do now. I can't explain the process; one day, years later, it just happened, but again, you have to want the change. That want is 90% of the process.

I think the issue of what my father said to me as a child was the last demon I had to face. He and I have a good relationship now. I can't come out and say I love him, but I can say I have more respect for him now than I ever have. I've grown a lot in prison and he's come to realize that. We can sit in a room together and carry on an intelligent conversation without getting pissed off at each other. I used to think I never needed a father, but I've come to realize I do. He's my father and I'm his son -- that will never change. We still have our differences and I doubt we'll ever see eye-to-eye. He's extremely homophobic, so I don't rub it in his face. On the other hand, I can talk to my mother about it anytime. She's constantly asking me if I've found Mr. Right yet. I tell her I'm holding out until I can marry a doctor.

Being gay in prison is not all fun and games. Sometimes it's dangerous. Gay men in prison are automatically labeled as "women," "punks" or "f--kboys." Homosexuals are looked at as a weaker class of human being. Some homosexuals were heterosexual before they came in, known as being "turned out" -- circumstance led to their homosexuality. Some homosexuals are commodities, playing a part in the economical structure mentioned earlier, being bought, sold, lost in card games, traded to pay off debts or what have you. Rape isn't reserved specifically for gay people. If you're pretty enough, it can happen to you, gay or straight. Masculine homosexuals such as myself are known as "bull queers" or "bandits." Those inmates with a lower mental state, thinking we all want to be women, refer to us as "daggers." Some, however, manage to find decent, loving, lasting relationships. I know couples who have been together for 10 or 15 years. I myself spent five wonderful years with a very kind, loving man. The relationship would have lasted longer, but he was transferred and I couldn't follow him. Now, years later, we still keep in touch and are the best of friends.

I'm not saying I had it easy. At first, I was preyed upon. Homosexuality in prison is looked upon as a weakness. Eventually you do what you have to do to prove you're not going to sit around and be bullied anymore; I'll skip the gory details and leave it up to your imagination. There isn't anything unique about being gay in prison. In the long run it will be what you allow it to be. There are times when I regret being out of the closet and there are times when I'm proud of it.

Eventually, I'll be released into a community which I am sure will not welcome me with open arms. In a time when more and more violent offenders are being required to register with police, reintegration is becoming more and more difficult. Hopefully, I'll find a community which won't be too quick to judge me by what I did, a community which will understand I have paid my debt and will give me the same respect they give each other. Maybe that sounds like Utopia, but that's what I hope. Once I'm out, staying out is totally up to me. I certainly don't plan on killing again; believe me, I really don't want to relive this.

As I go for my degree in Social Service, it's my goal and desire to work with kids who are as I was. My biggest fear is becoming institutionalized which, of course, I have to a certain degree. Prison is about programming and the trick is to become deprogrammed. Of all the things you may end up having while you're in prison, there is one thing you will never have -- responsibility. You don't have to worry about paying rent or where the next meal is coming from or when the next insurance payment is due. It will be so easy to know that all I have to do is violate my parole and I can escape all of life's responsibilities. I don't want that to happen to me.

I think what I will need most is someone who's been there. When I get out, I'm going to have feelings I may not know how to deal with, culture shock being one of them. If someone who has been through prison, gotten out, dealt with those same feelings and has succeeded is available for me to talk with, I'll be all right. I'll need someone who can relate to whatever I may go through. I don't know if I'll be able to handle all those new feelings on my own.

I'm 35 now. I'll probably be pushing 50 when I get out, if I get out. Whatever life I'm going to have, I'll have to build it on my own. My determination and my inner drive to succeed will aid me in remaining free. In addition, prison as a whole, my memories of what I have seen and survived, the riots, the murders, all of it will keep me from coming back. I hope.

Paul Everson left home at age 16 and worked the streets of Boston, then New York City, as a prostitute. The murder he committed in 1982 at age 18 earned him a minimum 25 year sentence which he is serving at the Maine State Prison. Paul is a writer of poetry, short stories, children's books, screen plays and screen play treatments. His poetry won the 1988 Golden Poet Award (World of Poetry), two Certificates of Award (Famous Poet Society) and the 1998 Award of Recognition and Diamond Homer Trophy (Famous Poet Society). Paul was co-creator, creative consultant and associate producer of the youth awareness/prevention documentary, "Choices: Stories from the Maine State Prison." His hope upon release is to go for a degree in Social Service and help children who are as he once was.

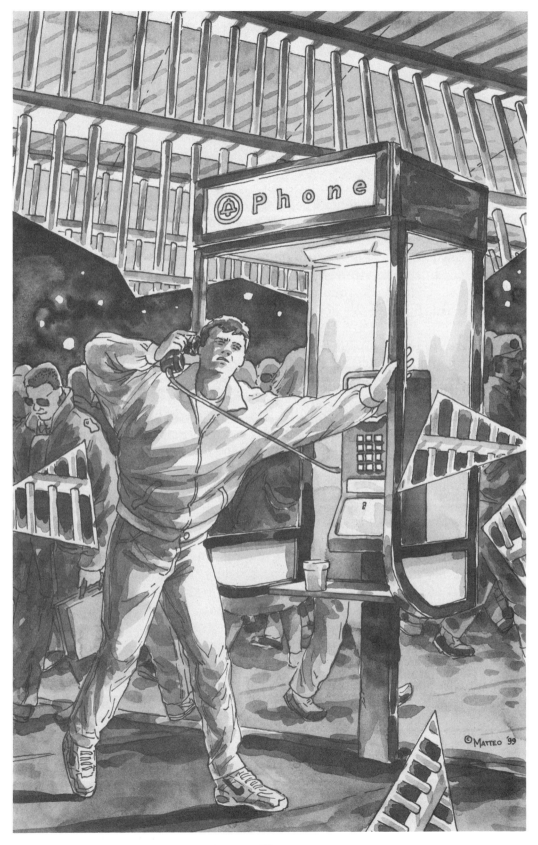

COUNSELING IN PRISON: A PERSONAL VIEW FROM INSIDE

Stephen Fraley

Counseling criminal offenders is challenging, to say the least, but it can also be extremely rewarding. People go into the counseling profession for various reasons, but I hope that most of them are driven by a simple and genuine desire to help others and to make life happier for as many people as possible. Burnout in this environment is certainly a real and pressing phenomenon, but fortunately I have managed to avoid it. After 18 years in prison and 11 years as an inmate counselor, I believe that I can speak from experience. But first, a little about myself.

I came to prison in 1981 for taking another young man's life in a street altercation. I was attacked by several individuals and shot one of them in my attempt to defend myself. I was convicted of murder and given 20 years to life in New York State Prison. As a certified paralegal assistant, I fought my case in the courts for 12 years. At first I believed that my imprisonment was totally unfair. Eventually, however, I came to see that my former lifestyle and behavior gave rise to my legal problems. The counseling that I received helped me to accept this.

My home life in North Carolina was dysfunctional. I am the ninth of 11 children. My father was alcoholic, irresponsible and violent. In my early teens, I began to associate with negative influences in my community. I wanted to be recognized and accepted -- negative attention was better than none at all. I started drinking, stealing, cutting class and fighting.

Since my father was such a poor provider, my mother had to work 12 hours a day to keep us afloat. This left little time for nurturing and disciplining. Mom tried her best, but I wouldn't listen to her or the few teachers who made an effort to reach me. No matter how much guidance they offered, the grip of the streets was too strong, and I ultimately had to return to my peers and the contrary influences they presented. I felt trapped.

My father needed Alcoholics Anonymous, but I never heard of such a program until I was grown. All of us needed family counseling because our value system had been so warped by his behavior. Our entire community needed intervention on a grand scale -- marriage counseling, family counseling, parenting classes, sex education, academic tutoring and after-school programs for children -- because there were literally hundreds of children who grew up the same way I did. Too many of them ended up dead, in jail or strung out on drugs and alcohol. Also, to continue the vicious cycle, many of them became parents without the benefit of marriage or any knowledge of parenting. It takes a village to raise a child.

My early behavior patterns continued, leading to the abuse of various drugs in an attempt to escape my depressing life, right up to the night of May 22, 1981. I was high, selling marijuana in a dangerous environment and carrying an unlicensed revolver. I was convinced for a long time that I had done nothing wrong; I wasn't hurting anyone, I told myself. I was bitter because I felt I had gotten a raw deal.

Only after honest introspection in counseling groups did I come to accept my responsibility in this whole ordeal. I put myself in harm's way. I lived a life that was bound to culminate in tragedy. I used drugs, which impair the mind, and I sold drugs, an irresponsible and dangerous activity. Guns are unnecessary and provide false confidence, often leading to disaster; they constitute an easy option when one is afraid, hurt or angry. Without the gun, I would not have even felt safe in that area and not have been there to be attacked.

The first step toward overcoming a behavioral or psychological problem is to recognize it. Then you must take responsibility for your acts, thoughts and emotions. We make choices in life and must accept the consequences thereof. Empowerment is not only a belief that you can do something right, but also a belief that you can avoid doing wrong. Counseling empowered me to believe that I can leave the old Stephen behind and live up to my God-given potential.

Moved by the relief and freedom of my own healing, I became a counselor myself and in that found my niche. I also teach and write, but my main goal in life, the work that rewards me and nourishes my own growth the most, is helping others through counseling. I pray for the opportunity to do this kind of work upon my release. This and the support of family, friends and groups will help keep me moving in the right direction. No matter what struggles I face, I will never come back to prison!

Over the years, I have been involved in many counseling groups, as participant and facilitator. Experiencing the process from both perspectives is an advantage, because it allows me, as a counselor, to empathize more readily with my clients. It is not true, however, as some suggest, that therapists cannot be effective with prisoners unless they have experienced the criminal lifestyle firsthand. Personal experience would certainly add to their understanding, but it is not a prerequisite. There are many genuine, caring and effective civilian therapists working with prison inmates.

I joined the <u>Drug Involvement Group (DIG)</u> in 1988 at Attica Correctional Facility. DIG had four sections at the time and they all stayed full. At least 90% of prisoners have been involved with drugs, either using, selling or doing crimes for money to buy them.

I was at work in the law library when a friend told me about DIG and suggested that I check it out. I said, "Yeah, why not? Maybe I have something to contribute based on my past experience." I hadn't used drugs since my arrest, because I knew that it had led to my predicament and I had to change my life or die a miserable failure. I was clean, yes, but I had not addressed the roots of my addiction.

The group was led exclusively by inmates -- guys I knew, guys like me. I sat with them for over a week without saying much. Many of their drug histories surprised me. I was impressed and frightened by their honesty. I was an intelligent, clean-cut fellow and no one knew about my prior drug abuse, a shameful part of my life that I never discussed. Eventually, I garnered enough courage to open up. It didn't come all at once, but in time I was able to tell "my story" without feeling like I wanted to cut and run, hide my face or return to the lie I used to live. This was the hardest work I'd ever done and the most rewarding. I faced my shame and guilt like a man and started to feel genuinely good about myself.

As a secondary gain, I realized that I was also helping others by openly facing my demons. I became a volunteer facilitator after graduating from the six-month program, and continued to grow, reach out to others in their struggles and dig into my own past for the roots of my addiction. I guess my experience with DIG gave me the counseling bug, because I immediately joined two other programs: Anger, Behavior and Communication (ABC) and Anger & Violence (A&V). These programs operated basically the same way as DIG.

In general, I learned in these groups how to express my anger in non-confrontational ways. We covered graphic descriptions of anger, communication skills, anger control techniques, role-playing of conflict scenarios (often recording them), stress and moral dilemmas. I later attended the Alternatives to Violence Project (AVP) which features three days of intensive anger management training.

I completed the Aggression Replacement Training for Peer Counselors/Trainers in 1990. In this program we covered conflict resolution, assertiveness training, structured learning of anger control skills and moral dilemmas, with a heavy dose of rehearsal and role playing. We assigned homework in virtually every topic and gave numerous oral and written examinations. Establishing solid group dynamics often seems unimportant to a beginning counselor, but he will ignore it at his own peril. Here are examples of techniques which encourage positive involvement of participants:

(1) Ask the participants to sit in a circle, which you will join. This allows everyone to see the eyes of everyone else, as eye contact is crucial to communication. The group should consist of 12 to 15 members. Make an effort to remember their names; this goes a long way toward building necessary rapport.

(2) After inviting the students to introduce themselves, give a program overview and acknowledge any diversity among the group members, based on their introductions; explain that it is a strength if they see themselves as a team over and above any differences, come to trust and rely on one another,

and address any misunderstandings or disagreements immediately and openly.

(3) Make sure the members understand that this group will be a team effort and everyone will be responsible for contributing. The work will be approached as a group, not a class. Remind the members periodically that this is their group; what they gain from it will depend, for the most part, on what they give.

(4) Make it clear to the group that you do not have all the answers, that human behavior is too complex for you to assume the role of the omniscient expert. You understand the material and have some counseling experience, of course, but you will be learning right along with the participants.

(5) If any group member has a problem with your format or approach, he should be invited to expound on it. All members should be allowed to respond if they would like. You should be willing to make slight changes that will not compromise the group's goal. Otherwise, you will politely summarize their comments and justify the necessity of the group structure. Stay alert for hidden agendas. When a group member has private, personal agendas that are contrary to the group's goals, he must be challenged and brought back into the fold. If that is not possible, then making everyone aware of it will seriously lessen the wayward member's success. In this way, it can become a real-life learning experience in how to deal with difficult people or challenges in general. A final option if his behavior becomes too much of a distraction is to remove him from the group.

Now, a word about counseling methods. You should use diverse and flexible methods to approach your group facilitating tasks, including psychodynamic techniques, person-centered therapy, behavior modification, rational-emotive therapy, lecture and discussion, and video and discussion. In the category of psychodynamic techniques, the client will be encouraged to talk openly about his past and to see the connections between childhood experiences and adult emotions and behaviors. As part of person-centered therapy, the counselor shows empathy and understanding to the client, without presuming to tell him directly how to solve his problems. Behavior modification is used by giving positive reinforcement in the nature of kind words, encouragement and affirmation, or by withholding them. Rational-emotive therapy involves challenging the irrational thoughts and beliefs of group members and offering more reasonable self-statements which are more adaptive in our society. In lecture and discussion sessions, usually supplemented by handouts, the counselor gives a very brief talk on a subject and then opens the group for rational discussion which he will facilitate. Video and discussion sessions involve showing a topical video, discussing the reactions of the group members and challenging irrational or self-destructive responses.

This kind of eclectic therapeutic approach is the most popular because it is the most effective. The diversity of methods allows the counselor to select the best parts of each and to maintain the flexibility to address human problems without getting locked into one specific way of perceiving them.

Alcohol and Substance Abuse Training (ASAT) is a popular program at Collins Correctional Facility and throughout the Department of Correctional Services (DOCS) because so many inmates have drug histories. I became an ASAT volunteer in the early 1990s while working at the Pre-Release Center in Attica Correctional Facility.

The program at Collins is staffed by experienced drug and alcohol counselors with various backgrounds in corrections and the private sector. They follow a comprehensive plan for treatment and recovery that is imaginative, compassionate, flexible and effective. They have put together a staff of dedicated and experienced inmate peer counselors who work extremely hard to see that the participants get everything the program has to offer. It provides three individual A.M. and P.M. groups, each running on six month cycles. Beginning to feel free starts here and now, not when the inmate is released. Ex-offenders who are unfamiliar with the subtle changes in society and who remain foggy-minded from drugs are in trouble. They may as well make an appointment with the prison tailor for refitting.

ASAT offers hope to those who are brave enough to work through their problems. Serious counseling can touch the real prison inside where substance abuse problems begin. ASAT participants can reach their ultimate potential if they choose. They can prove to themselves that racking up a stack of certificates is not what recovery is all about. Instead, it is about mapping out a plan for realistic goals, working those plans through to fruition and realizing personal growth.

Participants are encouraged to keep in mind as well that addressing their drug problems not only helps them; by extension, it heals broken families by replacing distrust and fear with love and respect. Staying clean will allow them to secure a healthy future for themselves and their families. This means joining a drug program on the street in order to sustain the recovery that they started in prison.

If an inmate has a substance abuse problem, he should get into drug therapy immediately. If he does his part, the program will do its part. He should know before-hand, however, that programs like ASAT are serious and demanding. If he wishes to play games or just "get over," he will soon learn that this nonsense is not tolerated.

As one ASAT program aide put it: "You need not be in the final stages of addiction to seek help. You only need to recognize that you're on the road to addiction and be willing to get off this dead-end street." The journey begins with an admission that you have a problem. Emotional, spiritual and intellectual growth can be yours. As can be heard in many ASAT groups: "It works if you work it."

I was the Drug Relapse Prevention program coordinator in 1997 here at Collins. Doing relapse prevention work was interesting in many ways, but the most unique and rewarding aspect of it was that I worked so closely with men fresh off the street. For this reason, the program allowed me to make a more direct impact on my community outside of prison than any other counseling job in the prison system.

"Relapse" was available as an opportunity to avoid losing work release status for using drugs or alcohol. It was started on December 1, 1992, after the DOCS acknowledged that drug abuse leads to most of our crime problems. The majority of prisoners who lose work release status do so as a consequence of their addictions.

Other DOCS programs, such as <u>Comprehensive Alcohol and Substance Abuse Training (CASAT)</u> and <u>Willard Treatment Center</u>, have the same stated goal: to address drug addiction with treatment, as opposed to non-rehabilitative incarceration, and to get participants back to their communities as soon as possible. According to the Department, this frees up scarce prison beds for more serious offenders, letting them hold those individuals with problems for which the answers are less clear.

An in-house study of Relapse Prevention found a success rate of 54% from September 1995 through April 1997 -- excellent results compared to other drug rehabilitation programs in and out of prison. Of the 46% who violated work release after completing the program, 38.5% went back to drugs and 3.3% abused alcohol. This clearly justifies the existence of alternative drug and alcohol treatment.

Relapse was an intensive eight-week program. We started with a thorough orientation, providing an overview of the program and reviewing two contracts the participants must sign. In the 40 weekdays that followed, we covered such topics as self-awareness, denial, honesty, addiction-disease progression, responsibility, decision-making, aggressive feelings, self-hate, hidden anger and violence. On the level of practical problems outside of prison, we talked about conflict, AIDS and parole issues. We covered family dysfunction issues -- fetal alcohol syndrome, domestic violence and adult children of alcoholics. We dealt with life skills such as parenting, employment and budgeting, coping with death and dying and stress management. And we taught about the physiology and psychology of all major drugs. Virtually all these discussion issues were reinforced and dramatized by therapeutic videos. Finally, we had an after-care workshop on Monday evenings to reinforce recovery.

In addition to six hours of counseling five days a week, Relapse involved substantial written homework, mid-term and final examinations. The tests were rigorous, but the participants almost always did well because we "made sure" they knew the material.

Each Thursday morning, we had a discussion on criminal thinking, facilitated by an ASAT counselor. He addressed any number of the thirty criminal thinking patterns in the package, such as resentment of authority, lack of remorse and self-centeredness. During this time, the Relapse staff met to share information, exchange feedback, conduct ongoing training and prepare for the following week.

We generally had highly motivated participants because they knew this was a one-shot deal. They were experiencing the reality of prison once again and they desperately wanted to return to their families and communities. Relapse Prevention was a dynamic, constantly growing pro-gram, one in which we learned as we went.

In January of 1998, the program relocated to the work release facilities where the participants are living at the time of their relapse. With this move, they did not experience the shock effect of coming back to prison, a harsh reminder of what they had to lose. We hope that they have continued the success that we experienced; thus far we haven't received any evaluative reports.

My incarceration limits my ability to effect changes in my community and society at large, but I do what I can from where I find myself. I joined a program called A Look for Alternatives (ALFA) in 1993 while at Attica Prison, and for four years it allowed me to make a difference. There are many such programs throughout the DOCS. They are generally called Youth Assistance Programs (YAP).

These programs were inspired by the documentary "Scared Straight," which aired in 1976. They are conducted by inmates for young people 13 to 21. We tell them that if they can relate to our past behaviors (abusing drugs, committing crimes and quitting school), then they are headed for prison, too -- unless they choose an alternative.

Prison inmates who are changing their own lives compose a huge resource that should be used more frequently to address the behavior problems of young people. We know what they are faced with. We can relate to them in a more realistic way than their teachers, counselors and perhaps their parents.

"Scared Straight" is a well-known program and approach, but we don't use intimidation, threats or humiliation. We use compassion, understanding and respect to show the youths that we care what happens to them. With all due respect to "Scared Straight" for originating the idea of bringing young people into the prison setting for a dose of reality, we do not believe that we can scare anyone into doing the right thing. The motivation must come from inside in order for the changes to last. We give it to them straight and allow them to make their own decisions. Either way, we stress, a decision will be made: "You'll choose to change or eventually a judge will choose to remove you from society."

Not only do we discuss the behavior of prisoners, but also the buildings, grounds and routines. The topics include crime, drugs, prison realities, school and family. We discuss the lack of privacy, humiliation, loneliness, prison rules, violence, homosexuality, food, housing, recreation yards and the lack of pets, cars and often trees. Nobody in his right mind would choose a life of crime.

We tell them our names, ages, sentences, family backgrounds and criminal histories. For example, I tell them that I started getting into trouble when I was 12. I cut classes, stole cigarettes and liquor from my father, hung out with an older crowd, stole from stores and fought a lot. I wouldn't listen to anyone and it got worse throughout my teens. At 18, I tried weed. Six months later, I was selling and using heroin. I was certainly not in my right mind; I could have benefited from ALFA. In my 20's, I did every kind of drug that was available and did various crimes to support my addictions. At 28, I killed a man, and this was connected to the lifestyle I had chosen.

I've changed a lot since then. The man that I am today is nothing like the loser who came to prison 18 years ago. I've learned my lesson, but my message to the youths is that this is no place for them to learn theirs.

If society can supplant its general distaste for prisoners, we can do a lot more to reverse our nation's devastating crime problems, particularly with regard to young people. As a national community, we need to pay more attention to them before, rather than after, they are incarcerated.

I am an active member of the Community Awareness Program (CAP) which meets once a week. Three inmate volunteers comprise the orientation panel which addresses questions related to crime, the criminal justice system and prison. Our diversity plays an integral part in our message, representing backgrounds in urban, suburban and rural America. Each of us shares his crime and prison experience. Unlike ALFA or YAP, this program simply provides information to high school students who are taking classes in criminal justice, political science and business law. This way, if any of these students take a job in corrections, they'll start with a realistic notion of the system. If they choose some other career path, it will help them to have an understanding of crime and corrections which is, unfortunately, a big part of our culture.

Now, the Cephas program is something else altogether. Cephas, a Greek word which means foundation stones, is a prisoner restoration group that was founded by Harold Steele after the tragic Attica prison rebellion of 1971 in which 43 men died. Steele had been a construction supervisor for Eastman Kodak, but was inspired to dedicate his life to prison ministry with a mission to help prisoners transform their lives and learn how to be productive members of society. Through the years, the organization with headquarters in Rochester and Buffalo, has expanded to other Western New York prisons: Albion, Orleans, Wyoming and Collins. Whereas the state recidivism rate among prisoners is often as high as 50%, only 30% of those paroled to Cephas ever return to prison. The key to the effectiveness of Cephas is that the program is holistic. That is, it addresses the entire life and lifestyle of its members -- in and out of prison -- rather than treating each problem individually. Most rehabilitation programs are geared toward single issues, such as drug abuse, alcoholism, violence, sexual abuse and AIDS/HIV. Cephas deals with all of these, the connections between them and all other aspects of life. Moreover, while we do not seek to indoctrinate members into any religion, we focus strongly on spiritual development. Cephas seeks to transform the entire person rather than simply eliminate the "problem behavior."

In my own life, I not only abused drugs, but I manipulated, lied and abused people. I had been clean for eight years when I joined Cephas in 1990, but rejecting the use of drugs was only the beginning. On a more basic level,

Cephas has helped me to address the fundamental causes of my addiction -- spiritual emptiness, low self-esteem and alienation.

In order to help our members to do the necessary work on themselves, we have to establish trust. In this sense, Cephas is much more than a prison rehabilitation group. It is a family. The family atmosphere makes us feel safe and loved so that we can more easily be open and honest about out thoughts, emotions and behaviors. Once a prisoner (or non-prisoner) reaches this point of self-acceptance, he is well on his way to self-transformation.

Cephas is in the business of remaking people and that goes far beyond mere rehabilitation. Before joining Cephas, I had already taken advantage of virtually all available therapy programs in the prison. I realized immediately that Cephas was different. Unlike other groups, in Cephas I found a home for life. I've been a Cephas member for 10 years and advisor to the Board of Directors for four years. In the early days, I was planning to live and work at Cephas, which also provides residences in Buffalo and Rochester for parolees. That will not be possible now, however, because a few years ago the parole department stopped allowing parolees to relocate to any area outside the city in which they were convicted. Notwithstanding this disappointment, my wife and I will enjoy a whole new life together because we have embraced the philosophy and principles of Cephas. I will also miss the employment and housing assistance that Cephas offers, but I am making other contacts.

Another organization which has brought spiritual growth to untold numbers is Kairos. Kairos is a nondenominational Christian organization with an international scope. Much of their work is done in prisons. They have four retreats per year plus weekly groups for those who have previously attended a retreat.

I attended a Kairos Christian retreat for four days in March, 1999. I had a spiritual awakening and religious conversion to Christianity, embracing Jesus Christ as my Lord and Savior. What were my spiritual beliefs before, you might ask. I believed in God and left it at that -- nice, simple and neat. It was strictly between us. Religion, including Christianity, was only a way to connect with God ... for those who needed it. I didn't and avoided the whole controversy of which religion is right by not choosing at all. (It is more complicated, of course, but this is not the place for a complete monograph on my erstwhile "Godianism.") My "Godianism" brought me a long way and helped me to transform my life while incarcerated. I became spiritually isolated, however, and had no one by which to measure my progress and no one to provide me spiritual guidance. At Kairos, it struck me that I needed a religious community with which to share my journey and to help me to the next level.

I decided to give Jesus a chance. This openness to Him quickly became a commitment to embrace Him. Only then did I realize that I had begun to stagnate and lose focus of my true mission -- to serve.

As a counselor, teacher and writer, I try to reach people in a way that will improve their lives. In my zeal to be productive, however, I had started to avoid the very people for whom I am doing the work. Dealing with some of my fellow inmates can be stressful, but that's no excuse. Since my conversion, I am becoming more available to others and Christ-centered. It's beautiful, and the interpersonal results are rewarding and reinforcing.

I agree with those who believe that we need a new approach to prisoner rehabilitation, but we must come up with credible suggestions. In some cases, counseling programs in prison primarily focus on eliminating criminal behavior, rather than considering the inmate's emotional background which is usually the origin and root of his criminality. Prison counseling programs usually lack a holistic therapeutic approach which is unfortunate, but inmates must seek out what they need elsewhere like responsible adults. Although prison systems are currently not equipped to address them, many volunteer programs, focusing on counseling as well as religion, can satisfy our spiritual needs.

Maybe we should consider restorative justice. This approach would restore both the offender and the victim to wholeness, using various methods, (e.g. restitution, victim and offender mediation, reconciliation meetings, holistic counseling and community service).

Some counseling programs in prison play a numbers game. Their success is not determined by how many inmates actually improve (which could be measured by recidivism rates), but by how many graduate. The problem is often inflexible policies which dictate the approach and duration of programs, forcing an unrealistic and ineffective structure upon the counselors. Even in the face of these bureaucratic challenges, however, the best counselors find a way to reach their clients.

Some inmates argue that counseling in prison is not worthy of the name. My 11 years as an inmate-counselor in New York State tells me that this is basically a generalization apparently intended to rationalize personal failure. I certainly sympathize with them, but overstating the case only calls our credibility into question. So let's keep it real. Most inmates who fail to get treatment choose to drop out or not to attend at all because they refuse to address their issues. On rare occasions, men who resist treatment are kicked out of programs because they become disruptive and interfere with the progress of others.

One way to avoid the recalcitrant client is to make program attendance strictly voluntary. That way, no one is forced to participate against his will. The difficulty with this is that many inmates need these programs to improve their chances for parole release, so they will attend even if they hate the idea.

Some detractors of prison counseling programs argue that the success rates are due to heavy doses of fear and intense supervision. Actually, the level of fear and supervision a client experiences is correlated with his resistance to change. He is closely supervised because he has proven untrustworthy, and he is afraid because he's smart enough to know that his stubbornness has consequences. Furthermore, 90% of the actual counseling in prison therapy groups (in New York) is done by inmate peer counselors, and they generally give fellow inmates the benefit of the doubt. The group participant must be responsible and demonstrate his motivation to change.

As a counselor, I know the challenge (and impossibility) of helping someone who doesn't want to be helped, of saving someone who doesn't want to be saved. Inmates and others in need of counseling bear a heavy responsibility in the therapeutic process. They must be open and willing to do the hard work necessary for change and growth.

The counseling that I have received in prison, as well as the spiritual development, changed my life. When arguing against exaggerated criticism of prison counseling programs, as I do here, one may leap to the conclusion that I support the status quo. Let me be clear: we need new approaches to rehabilitation. But we also need to remain credible, not taking indiscriminate potshots at existing programs, if we hope to gain the support of those who could make changes happen. Most of all, we need to be courageous, open-minded and creative.

Stephen Fraley, a counselor, teacher and writer, earned his B.S. in 1989 at Canisius College while incarcerated. He is certified with the New York State Department of Labor for 4,000 hours of apprenticeship training as a counselor and 2,000 hours as a teacher. He designed and initiated a new training class for counselors in 1993, the Group Counseling Workshop, and taught group counseling skills from 1993 to 1998. He is the author of <u>Community Preparation Workbook</u> (Biddle Publishing Co.), a counseling guide for basic transitional skills and constructive behavior, and is Editor of <u>Pen & Ink</u>, a prison newspaper. Stephen is widely published in professional journals, magazines, newspapers and books, picking up a number of awards along the way. He is incarcerated at Collins Correctional Facility and will be eligible for parole in 2001. He hopes to earn his Ph.D. in psychology upon release and to continue the work he is doing in prison.

THE VALUE OF ART IN PRISON

Christian Snyder

Let's face it, there is not a whole lot that's positive about being sentenced to, and serving time in, prison. Prison is a brutal environment with frequent assaults, razor cuttings or stabbings between prisoners, and physical confrontations between prisoners and corrections staff; any of these can result in serious injury to both parties. The long term psychological damage to the prisoner and the negative affect it has on his family is devastating.

Increased lockdown time and diminishing programs, which include the termination of college programs, has set the stage for punitive justice. This has helped to create an environment where frustration and boredom among the incarcerated can lead to increased negativity and counter-productive behavior.

For many individuals, reading books, watching TV and working out in the yard are not enough to stimulate the mind or occupy the many hours of the many years a prison sentence consists of. But it can be both rewarding and beneficial to incarcerated men and women to indulge in a hobby, whether it be in the form of crafts, sculpturing, composing and playing music, writing, drawing or painting in its many forms.

As an incarcerated artist myself, it is my goal to outline what I feel are the values of art in prison. My declarations are based on my direct observations of other men I have served time with and other prisoners whose success I'm aware of through reading about them and seeing their work published. I particularly want to share how my own life has been transformed by immersing my time and energy in art for the last seven years.

Developing or improving artistic talent behind bars consumes time -- lots of time. This investment of time can serve to steer one clear of the many "trap-offs" and potential for trouble that exists in a prison environment. Too much idle time fosters boredom, a sense of utter hopelessness and eventually deep despair. That may sound extreme, but I've seen it happen. Being in this frame of mind can lead a prisoner to make a single or series of bad decisions that can result in terrible consequences.

Indulging in an artistic hobby in prison can soothe an individual, bringing him enjoyment and inner peace. It offers a person a profound sense of satisfaction and an outlet for self-expression. Prison is not a place that is usually conducive to healthy self-expression, but having the opportunity to channel individual drive and creative energy into art projects satisfies this basic human need.

The rehabilitative values of having art flourish in prison are evident when we explore how creating art can boost a prisoner's self esteem and sense of personal worth. Developing one's artistic skills in any medium can build self-confidence and fuel a passion that can change personal values, behavior, even alter the course of someone's life.

I do not profess this lightly. The incarcerated artist can spend just a few or many years locked away. Hopefully, during this time, the emergence of a new focus and total redirection of goals for the future can occur. In the artistic realm, it's difficult to obtain an exact measure of success. It is relative to many things, most importantly to the individual artist's goals and outlook. I will, however, make the assertion that when a prisoner continues a hobby, witnessing the evolution and progression of talent, that person will see that headway and accept it as empirical proof of accomplishment and success. This in turn acts as an incentive to continue this form of productive enjoyment. This powerful element of motivation can be the catalyst to institute the monumental change in the priorities of a prisoner's life that I speak of.

When prisoners elicit interest in their work from their peers, it is another big step. Occasionally their work gets published, exhibited in an art show or purchased by a publishing firm or individual collector; these are all steps up the wonderful ladder of personal success. Again, with that sense of pride and accomplishment resulting from doing a pastime a prisoner enjoys, it will trigger more inspiration to strive to climb further up this ladder. The resulting benefit of gradual personal growth and development is probably the single most valuable element of salvation one can experience or generate from within themselves.

Involvement in arts and crafts can cause a prisoner to rediscover himself and undergo a metamorphosis in character, insight and sense of what is important in his life. This change of priorities occurs through the development of a love and passion for creating art. This type of involvement acts as a meaningful substitute and fills a void in the person who was caught up in the desperate lifestyle of committing crimes and battling substance abuse.

Art doesn't cure alcoholism or drug addiction. It doesn't remove the desire to commit crimes. An individual must want to change his lifestyle and change himself. Incorporating art in one's lifestyle is but one tool to be utilized in the process of journeying down a road that leads in the opposite direction from crime and self-destruction.

Let's look at artistic talent and potential. With the different forms of illustrative art, there exists a population of tremendously gifted men and women in our nation's penitentiaries. I have seen men behind bars render portraits in colored pencils and pastels of family members, even celebrities, that are flawless. I have seen magnificent watercolor and ink illustrations and pencil and charcoal sketches that are comparable to the best magazine illustrations on the market today. As far as oil paintings, I have seen masterpieces of landscapes, contemporary and abstract, aerial battle scenes and prison scenes that have generated an intense interest by serious art collectors and gallery owners. When these types of people gravitate toward a prisoner's art, I think it speaks volumes of the aesthetics and the caliber of his work.

Many prisoners are involved in making greeting cards that are suitable for any occasion, employing original, clever ideas that any greeting card company could benefit from. I have been in awe of the intricacy of some of the three dimensional pop-up cards that many hours went into to craft by hand.

Cartooning is a powerful, poignant and humorous artistic and intellectually creative form of expression that has a universal appeal to all. There are numerous very talented political and humor cartoonists in America's prisons today. I see their work published on a regular basis and they are masters at what they do. If these individuals continue to pursue cartooning as a career upon their release, there is no doubt in my mind that they will continue to succeed at a passion that many of them probably used their prison time to develop. If you explore this possibility in this context, developing one's artistic capabilities and gaining experience in the field while incarcerated constitute a powerful form of self -rehabilitation.

I stated that I am an incarcerated artist. To be specific, I am a cartoonist. I entered prison for the first time in 1993 and soon realized that the time I had to do was not going to go by quickly. I felt that I needed to find something constructive to do and to have the time I spent doing it in prison work to my advantage when I got released. I ended up coming full circle back to a talent that I had always possessed which is thinking of and drawing cartoons.

I have been successful at it. My work has been published in numerous books, magazines and professional trade journals. My cartoons have been on the Internet and exhibited in art shows in major cities across the country. I have been told by friends, editors and some of the top cartoonists in the profession that I have what it takes to make it as a top level cartoonist.

I'll be the first to say that I wish I had not broken the law and been sent to prison. However, those are the events which transpired and I cannot change that. What's important is the fact that I used what I like to term "down time" to develop my talent, gain valuable experience in cartooning and reach for my dream. I am grateful that I have been able to have access to art while behind bars and, to be fair, I know many prison facility administrators share my views of the rehabilitative values of having art programs in our prisons. Cartooning has enabled me to form definite goals as to what I want to pursue as at least one line of work upon my release. My drawing has been the center of my self-generated rehabilitative process. It has given me direction in my life that I did not possess prior to coming to prison.

I am confident that if I stay locked into pursuing my goals, I will not be returning to prison. If I can enjoy the success at cartooning that I have had in prison, I know that level of success will increase exponentially once I am released. Isn't that what it's all about, or should be all about -- prisoners

© 1999 CHRISTIAN SNYDER

finding ways to change their lives for the better which will enable them to make it on the outside without committing more crimes and returning to prison? Once released, even if a person only indulges in his art as a part time hobby so it consumes his time and prevents the involvement of negative activates, isn't that a victory for everyone?

There are other values of producing art in prison that are not associated with the arena of professional publishing or monetary gain. Art and craft projects given as gifts to friends and family members are a priceless symbol of love and dedication. The time spent on a project to be presented as a gift is, in effect, a way of conveying the message: "My time spent on this work is dedicated to you and is a symbol of my effort to change my life for the better."

Such a gift can be a bridge to mend broken relationships between a prisoner and his wife and children. Art as a gift represents a momento that is a keepsake and a reminder of the absent loved one who is behind bars. Art that is donated by prisoners to hospitals, schools and other public and community locations serves to enhance the public awareness of the value of art. Great art will always live on; whether the creator of such works is a prisoner or not should not hold any bearing on the cultural value or the public appreciation.

In some facilities, art is sold to the public through annual events sponsored by correctional departments. A percentage of sales goes towards restitution for victims and their families. These agencies have accounts that provide services and financial aid to victims of crime so that they may obtain counseling, or restore damaged or stolen property.

For the prisoner that feels this type of involvement is a way of repaying society for some of the carnage that he may have caused in his crime sprees, being able to donate part of his money received from art sales toward this cause is a positive step. Personal actions such as this further reinforce the concept that having art exist behind bars can contribute to individual growth, development and rehabilitation.

There is the reality that many prisoners involved in creating art will never be released. Also, not every artist behind bars will become a professional artist -- that is by no means the most valuable measure of accomplishment. Personal satisfaction and a strong sense of well being and inner peace is what every artist should strive for. It's a spiritual thing, really.

Art is not a cure-all for the troubles I or anyone else has. It will not solve all the problems that exist in our prisons, nor will it decrease the level of crime in our communities. It does, however, hold an important place in all levels of our society and it has healing and recovery potential.

It's a sad reality that many prisons are eliminating art programs and forbidding their inmates to purchase their own supplies. The justification given may be budget cuts, downsizing of programs or security concerns. It is also apparent that taking away such programs is a punitive action, designed to impress upon the public that institutions and politicians are being "tough on crime."

Unfortunately, many artists behind bars are currently experiencing the stifling of creativity by harsh punishment doled out by correctional departments. I don't see any good coming from these actions. It is necessary to ensure tools and supplies used in art hobbies are not used to injure staff and inmates. However, to simply yank away art supplies and programs and deny the incarcerated the opportunity to use time productively by engaging in peaceful, enjoyable pastimes -- just to appease an "outraged" and often uninformed public, or to break the spirit of an incarcerated artist -- is an act of vindictiveness.

Denying positive alternatives to violence, drug use and the bleakness of everyday prison existence simply increases the likelihood that these elements will flourish within our prison walls. Art is one of those valuable options that can and will steer one more imprisoned person away from those pitfalls if it is continued to be made available to him.

The channeling of raw talent and creative energy to produce a tangible form of unique art has been an integral part of our cognizance and our history. Art has defined our existence on this planet and become our legacy. It should make no difference if a person is free or will live out part or all of his remaining days in a cage. The human value of the creation of art is immeasurable; contained in that immeasurability is the value of art in prison.

Christian Snyder *is serving a 5-15 year sentence in New York State. He also served 4 years in the Marine Corps, with an honorable discharge, and earned an Associate Degree from Clinton Community College, graduating with high honors. His cartoons have been published in* <u>Frontiers of Justice</u> *(Volumes 1 and 2). Since his incarceration, Chris has launched a career as a freelance magazine and editorial cartoonist; his work has appeared in a huge variety of publications, specializing in everything from fish to cigars. He plans to continue this profession upon his release.*

JUDGE ME WHEN I AM FREE

Vincent Johnson

Ending it all

Is it all right
If I take my life
And throw it away
To the outside
world?
Can I
Take a sharp
Turn
And cut the corner
Of prison life
Leaving my cell to bleed
Emptiness?
Painful, loveless, futureless place
Somebody please help me
End it all
Help me overdose
On a tall glass of pure
Freedom.

A Memory

Had a friend named Deondre
Back in 1979.
He was a big football fan,
Knew everything about it,
Used to call me Vince Sculley
And when we played rumble
With a ball of paper on the USC campus
With our pant legs in our socks
And balled paper in our shirts for
shoulder pads,
He'd pretend to be every player with fame
As we all called out their names
Running for the goal:
"Franco Harris," "Mean Joe Green," "Tony Dorsett"
"Charles White," "Roger Stauback."
We knew and were them all.

Not My Parents

When I was a child
I was abused,
chained and over-punished,
starved, neglected, deprived,
and I tell of my abuse at times
and people stare
as if to say: "Poor thing,
what awful parents he must have."
But they don't know
that my abusers were of
The California Youth Authority
at the hands of the state.
This for nearly a decade
had nothing on a home whipping.

I Saw Inside a Poet's Head

Like in a child's toy box,
Like in a scrap yard and a manufacturing plant,
I saw inside a poet's head
The scrap of uncomposed poems,
Verses that haven't left the image stage,
Frozen thoughts with strange characteristics:
A jetliner falling toward the earth with all 268
Passengers ejecting to safety;
To the left lies a river with no name,
Killer whales bask on the banks waiting for
Composition with killer grins;
In the distance a waterfall drops from a cluster of clouds,
Filling the souls of manifesting kings;
Behind me flashes a quick glimpse of hell,
A crowd fleeing tumbling flames as a burning pheasant,
caught in the crossfire, screeches by;
Miles ahead an iceberg rests atop a puffing volcano.
I wish for results, but the thoughts lie unactivated.
By nightfall, I look to the sky to catch the
clash of two armies that took their fight to the moon
To leave earth at peace.
In another part of the sky drifts star-bright words that
Fall one by one to the image-filled earth, only to
Roll down inky hill of ball point pen.

Stifled

To want me with no children
To want me with no wife
To want me with no freedom
Is to want me with no life

They tell me these things are needless
Yet they have them all.

Missing California

Golden hills, emerald lawns
Northern grapes and southern palms
One half dome, one golden gate
How I miss that golden state
Place of birth that cradled me
West L.A. but east of sea
Hawks by day and owls by night
Birds of prey my favorite sight
What a place so sweet and warm
Disneyland, Knott's Berry Farm
Freedom fighters, many parks
How the absence breaks my heart
Little children run at play
With laugher dashing every way
Gospel echoes through the air
Spanish springing everywhere
California's calling me
To watch the sunset dive at sea
To view the mountains decked with trees
And feel the western desert breeze
To hear the coyotes howl by night
And see the crows and gulls in flight

But Iowa's cold is home to me
Until this prison sets me free.

The Unworthy

Thirteen years ago today
my father passed away,
a veteran of World War II,
he died poor with hardly enough to be buried.
Can you imagine me belly-chained and shackled,
escorted down the busy boulevard of central
in Los Angeles?
In my fresh Ventura outfit,
I stood over silence in silence.
Ashamed to cry before the guard,
I halted hot tears at the borders of my eyes.
Five years later I was finally freed from Preston,
three dollars and a bus ticket to L. A.
-- that's all I was worth?
You mean after all those riots and fights,
after all that jerking off and crying,
after all the fear, missed youth and longing for hope,
all I earned was three dollars and a swift
kick in the pants?
The unworthy!

Mistaken Identity

They tell her I have someone
But I don't
They say I'll be a cheater
But I won't
They hint I'll be abusive
A lie
They say that I'm no good for her
But why?
I pant and I pace and I try to keep cool --

It's V.J. (I rage), not O.J., you fools!

Off From Work

You cannot judge the mechanic
in oil stained work clothes
saying that you will never eat with him.
You cannot judge the wet and smoky fireman,
saying that you will not sleep with him.
You cannot judge the muddy child at play
saying that you will never hug him,
nor can you judge the caged frantic bird,
saying that it's too wild to be free,
or the armed soldier at war,
saying that he's too violent for love
when all is shed in the march homeward.
So how can you judge me
in my prison occupation?

Judge me when I am free,
off from the work of hating prison.

Vincent Johnson *is originally from California, but is incarcerated in the Iowa State Prison for the robbery of two pizzas. He has been writing poetry since 1988 and received several Certificates for his work, as well as being published in several small press anthologies. He is the author of two chapbooks of poetry, including* <u>Iowa On the Inside</u> *(Audenreed Press). He hopes to return to California on his release.*

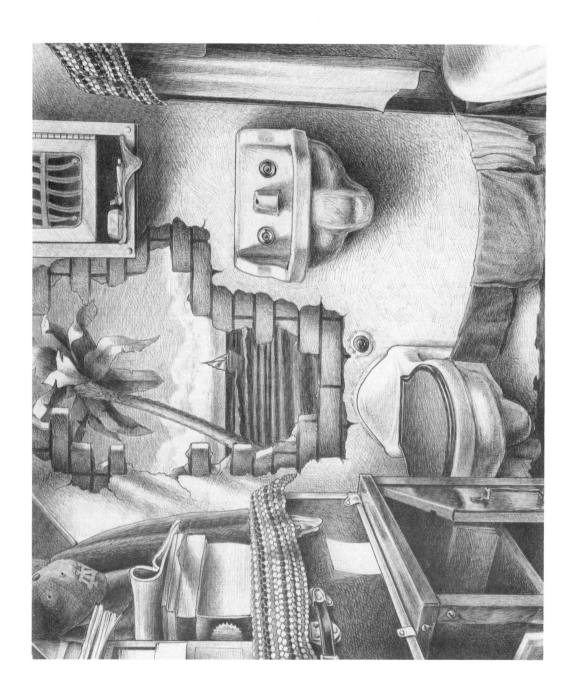

TRIALS OF INNOCENTS*

Dennis J. Dechaine

Mankind censure injustice fearing that they may be the victims of it, and not because they shrink from committing it. Plato, The Republic, 3rd century B.C.

Imagine being a 21-year-old with numerous prospects and suddenly having your world turned upside down by accusations of murder. Imagine being forced to stand before a jury of your peers while a parade of state witnesses spew inaccurate and vituperative testimony, painting the portrait of a monster you cannot begin to identify. Imagine being wrongly convicted and sent to death row to await your execution by a justice system that is blind even to truth. For Kerry Max Cook, to have had the luxury of imagining that fate would have been a dream come true; instead, he lived that nightmare and his conviction was just the beginning of a 22-year pain-filled ordeal that the average human would not have survived.

It was 1978 when Kerry was convicted of the particularly brutal murder of Linda Jo Edwards, a 21-year-old secretary from Tyler, Texas. "One day I'll prove I didn't do it," Cook told a reporter after his conviction. "If it takes me 10 years, 20 years, I'll prove I didn't do it."[1]

Kerry Cook arrived at Ellis I penitentiary near Huntsville in July of 1978 and was housed in one of the segregated cell blocks reserved for death row inmates. Shortly after he arrived, Kerry was savagely raped by three other prisoners who finished their degrading assault by carving a lewd comment on his buttocks with a razor blade. In those early days on death row, Kerry recalls that the loneliness was nearly as bad as the abuse. He would often think of his family and burst into tears. Even through a degrading prison indoctrination, Kerry focused on the fight to correct the wrongs imposed on him by the State of Texas. He soon learned that the urgency he felt in getting back into court was not shared by the Texas judiciary. It was 1991 before Kerry's second trial was granted on the basis of constitutional violations, and that trial resulted in a hung jury. A third trial in 1994 resulted in a conviction and another death sentence, but by this time the media were beginning to pay attention.

[*Editors' Note: The essays in this volume are written in the first person by those who openly admit their involvement in the crimes that sent them to prison. This essay, "Trials of Innocents," is an exception; the editors felt it was important to include a contribution on behalf of the many men and women in this country who are serving time for crimes they did not commit.]

In 1996, the Texas Court of Appeals again overturned Kerry's conviction, this time citing "prosecutorial and police misconduct has tainted this entire matter from the outset."[2] Kerry was released on a bond paid for by friends who had joined the fight to prove his innocence. The district attorney, however, vowed to seek the death penalty for a fourth time.

In a late August 1999 article in the <u>Dallas Observer</u>(on-line), a journalist said that Cook spent 17 years on death row thanks to Smith County prosecutors and cops who fibbed, connived and bent rules to put him there. Even the conservative <u>Dallas Morning News</u> joined the fray. An investigative reporter named David Hanners repeatedly accused Smith County prosecutors of railroading Cook by building its case on "circumstantial, prejudicial, questionable and conveniently altered evidence."[3] In his first trial, prosecutors had gone so far as to welcome the testimony of a prison informant with the nickname "Shyster" to help them secure Kerry's execution.

Despite a trail of prosecutorial impropriety, the county again succeeded in indicting him, and trial was scheduled for early 1999. However, before a jury was picked, prosecutors made Kerry an offer: in exchange for a face-saving (theirs) no contest plea, he would serve no more prison time. He was given a half hour to decide. Just a few days earlier, the state crime lab in Austin had finally gotten around to testing semen stains found on the victim's underwear. Could it be that the DNA belonged to someone other than Kerry Cook?

While Kerry pondered the decision to trade his innocence for freedom, he was haunted by memories of death row. Imagine his frustration at having been wrongly convicted and thrust into the savagery of prison, unable to respond to violence in any manner that might undermine his pursuit of justice. Imagine the fear and vulnerability that must have come from being shackled by innocence. Yes, he took the deal. Who can blame Kerry for not wanting to return to an untenable situation, for not daring to jeopardize the miracle of his survival. After the deal was done, a party broke out, but all Kerry could do was sit apart from his friends, saddened by what he had been forced to trade for this moment. "This is not the victory I had envisioned for myself from a 5-by-9 cell," he said. "I am innocent, but convicted."[4]

Cook's lawyers have filed for a full pardon from Governor George Bush, but Kerry knows this will be an uphill battle. In December of 1999 he told a <u>Dallas Observer</u> reporter, "The prosecution nailed me to the wall. They sponsored perjury, suppressed evidence, manufactured a case out of whole cloth. It's madness .... I lived this nightmare for 22 years, but how am I supposed to tell my story without looking like a liar or like I'm making something up or hiding the truth? Who is going to believe me? Who is going to believe me?"[5] And what about the DNA test conducted 22 years after the crime? Results excluded Kerry Max Cook as the source of biological evidence found on the victim's clothing, further supporting his claim of innocence.

What happened to Kerry Cook teaches us that our vaunted American justice system tends to reflect the imperfection of its participants. Unfortunately, the Cook case is just one of many where innocent people have been convicted of crimes they never committed. In 1987, Hugo Bedau and Michael Radelet published a revealing and controversial study in the <u>Stanford Law Review</u> regarding that most irrevocable of all punishments -- the death penalty. According to the authors, in this century at least 350 people have been wrongfully convicted of capital crimes (or potentially capital crimes) and 23 have been executed.[6]

Given the strong support for capital punishment in America, the study was attacked on several fronts. In the fall of 1988, the <u>Stanford Law Review</u> published a response to the Bedau-Radelet study. The authors of the response, Stephen Markman, Assistant Attorney General for the U.S. Department of Justice, and Paul Cassell, Assistant Attorney General for the Eastern District of Virginia, based their rebuttal in large part on the sufficiency of trial evidence that resulted in the convictions and executions of people that Bedau-Radelet claimed were actually innocent. Though Markman and Cassell tried to diminish the Bedau-Radelet study by endeavoring to prove the guilt of some people whose cases had been overturned on appeal, they nevertheless deigned to offer the following insight:

"Given the fallibility of human judgments, the possibility exists that the use of capital punishment may result in the execution of an innocent person. This terrible prospect raises the issue of whether the risk of error in administering the death penalty is sufficiently high both to outweigh the potential benefits of capital punishment and to offend the moral sensibilities that must support a free society's criminal justice system."[7]

Just how often has the death penalty been used to kill innocents, inadvertently or otherwise, in the history of our country? In 1608, George Kendall had the misfortune of being the first person executed in America. Kendall, who was a governing councilor in what is now Virginia, was shot for being a spy. Walt Espy, a leading researcher on the history of the death penalty, says that evidence indicates that Kendall was railroaded by angry opponents who wanted him removed from power.[8]

Espy estimates that as many as 22,500 people have been killed by states since the birth of our nation, and he adds that by 1984, of the 681 people executed in his home state of Alabama, at least 10 were found to be innocent after the fact.[9] By extrapolation, we can reasonably estimate that at least 300 innocents have been executed in the history of our country.

According to the Death Penalty Information Center in Washington, D.C., since the reintroduction of the death penalty in 1970, 78 innocent prisoners have been freed from death row, and we can only guess at how many are being left behind for the executioner.[10] The new millenium finds about 3,500 people on death row in America, compelling one to wonder if the numbers suggested by Bedau-Radelet will be dwarfed in the next century.

Despite the fact that law enforcement occasionally admits to the possibility of wrongful conviction, even in death penalty cases, arguments tend to arise over fundamental questions. How often does injustice occur? Why does it occur? What can be done to reduce its incidence? This essay attempts to address those questions.

In 1996, Professors C.R. Huff, Arye Rattner and Edward Sagarin fueled the wrongful conviction debate when they published their academic treatise, "Convicted but Innocent: Wrongful Conviction and Public Policy." Though there is no easy way to determine how many innocent people are convicted every year in the United States, the Huff study attempted to quantify the phenomenon by tabulating the results of 229 questionnaires returned by a cross section of criminal justice personnel in Ohio and 41 state Attorneys General. Due to the participants' backgrounds in the justice system, the results of the questionnaire are viewed as conservative by the authors of the study. Huff and his partners concluded that only one-half of one percent of all convictions result in injustice.[11] This figure represents only eight serious "index" crimes which include murder, non-negligent manslaughter, rape, aggravated assault, robbery, burglary, larceny-theft, motor vehicle theft and arson.

The wrongful conviction rate expressed in the Huff study, conservative though it may be, indicates that in 1993 around 10,000 wrongful convictions occurred in the United States and many more occurred if lesser crimes are included. (The Huff study referred to the Department of Justice Bureau of Justice Statistics estimate of 2.85 million people charged with index crimes in 1993.)

Another study worth noting when attempting to quantify the frequency of wrongful conviction was conducted by Kalven and Zeisel in 1966. Their research on the American jury involved the cooperation of a large number of judges. In this study, judges were asked to secretly render their own verdicts while awaiting jury decisions. In four percent of the cases, judges had voted not guilty when juries returned guilty verdicts. Were juries wiser than judges in these cases, or are thousands being wrongfully convicted every year by ill-informed jurors?

An even more alarming wrongful conviction rate came out of a 1996 Justice Department report entitled, "Convicted by Juries, Exonerated by Science: Case Studies in the Use of DNA Evidence to Establish Innocence After Trial." The report found that of the 8,048 rape and rape-and-murder cases referred to the Federal Bureau of Investigation crime lab from 1988 to 1995, fully 25% of arrestees were found to be not guilty on the basis of forensic(DNA) test results. Just a few years earlier, the majority of the wrongly arrested innocents represented in this report would have probably been sent to prison, their voices added to the chorus of prisoners clammering for justice.

It sometimes seems that conservatives view the wrongful conviction issue as the bailiwick of liberals who can better relate to the individual and social costs of injustice. Despite the incalculable suffering intimated by the most conservative of estimates, social costs are magnified when we consider that one of the inevitable consequences of wrongful conviction is the freedom afforded actual offenders to continue their criminality, without regard for the political inclinations of their victims.

It is not uncommon for claims of innocence by prisoners to be viewed by jaded media and law enforcement personnel as pathetic attempts by desperate criminals to avoid their comeuppance. But in the United States, no single aspect of forensic science is serving to support claims of innocence as demonstrably as genetic testing, a technology that identifies the DNA (deoxyribonucleic acid) left behind at crime scenes.

Human DNA is similar to a fingerprint in its individual uniqueness. A difference between DNA and fingerprints is that DNA is found in every cell of our bodies, increasing opportunities to discern the identity of a perpetrator at a crime scene. DNA evidence has been collected from unusual sources and in quantities so minute as to seem insignificant. Crimes have been solved by DNA analyses of the saliva left on cigarette butts, postage stamps and even ski masks. DNA testing of single strands of hair has solved other crimes as has the perspiration left on a baseball cap. DNA's forensic value is even more impressive when we consider that testing methods can yield results on evidence that is decades old.

We have come a long way since 1986 when DNA testing was first used to convict a man in Great Britain. The United States is now in the process of building DNA databases, and as the number of profiles increase, old murder and rape cases are being solved by the hundreds. Christopher Asplen, executive director of the National Commission on the Future of DNA Evidence, describes DNA as the "most reliable evidence."[12] The commission, made up of experts chosen by the National Institute of Justice, readily acknowledges the reliability of DNA testing as a forensic science. In an article in Reason magazine, Director Asplen stated that no other form of evidence for identifying human beings has gone through such rigorous scientific and legal validation as DNA has.[13] Just as DNA has been a forensic windfall to law enforcement, it has also been an unexpected source of hope for the wrongfully convicted.

In September of 1999, the U.S. Department of Justice published a report entitled, "Postconviction DNA Testing: Recommendations for Handling Requests." In the Introduction, U.S. Attorney General Janet Reno underscores the importance of DNA testing as a forensic tool, not only useful in convicting criminals, but also in freeing those who were wrongfully convicted. Her message states:

"The vigilant search for truth is the hallmark of our criminal justice system. Our methods of investigation, rules of criminal procedure and appellate process are designed to ensure that the guilty are apprehended and convicted while the innocent are protected. But while ours is a system to be cherished, it is not a perfect system, and those of us charged with the administration of justice have a responsibility to seek its continued improvement. These recommendations acknowledge and accept that responsibility. They were created because forensic DNA technology can strengthen our confidence in the judicial process.

In 1996, the National Institute of Justice (NIJ) issued the research report, 'Convicted by Juries, Exonerated by Science: Case Studies in the Use of DNA Evidence to Establish Innocence After Trial.' It told the stories of 28 men whose innocence was proven by applying DNA technology to evidence after they were convicted and sent to prison. They had, however, served an average of 7 years in prison. Since the publication of that report, more than 40 other cases have been identified.

In response to NIJ's report, I requested that the Institute establish a National Commission on the Future of DNA Evidence to identify ways to maximize the value of DNA in our criminal justice system. I commend the commission's recognition of the need to address the postconviction issue immediately and I applaud the vision of a better system that these recommendations provide.

The analysis offered by these recommendations applies DNA technology to the appeals process while recognizing the value of finality in the criminal justice system. Where DNA can establish actual innocence, the recommendations encourage the pursuit of truth over the invocation of appellate time bars. In those cases in which DNA testing may be determinative of innocence, the recommendations encourage cooperation between prosecutors, defense attorneys, laboratories and the judiciary. Likewise, in those cases in which a DNA exclusion would be of no value in the determination of actual innocence, the recommendations discourage the filing of a DNA-based appeal simply because the attorney's client requested it.

I encourage prosecutors, defense attorneys, the judiciary, victim advocates and laboratory personnel to apply these recommendations to their individual cases. Using DNA technology fairly and judiciously in postconviction proceedings will help those of us responsible for the administration of justice to do all we can to ensure a fair process and just result."[14]

In her message, AG Reno recognizes that many criminal cases exhausted legal remedies before the advent of DNA testing, and for the sake of truth, the conventional time limitations imposed by the courts should be relaxed to take advantage of new technologies. Hundreds, if not thousands, of innocent people in prison are hoping that these recommendations will finally yield justice, that their cases will be fully heard and the truth revealed, despite the adversarial system of justice that sometimes loses sight of its responsibility to pursue truth.

"The biggest problem with the commission's recommendations," says Peter Neufeld, Director of the Innocence Project, "is that they are only recommendations. Prosecutors don't have to follow them if they don't want to."[15] Neufeld directs the Cardozo School of Law Innocence Project with Barry Scheck, and both men know all too well the legal and political hurdles that prevent promising technology from being used to free innocent prisoners.

The Innocence Project's mission is to assist prisoners in using DNA technology to prove their innocence. The project performs legal triage to deal with the volume of requests it receives. In 1999, approximately 200 cases were actively pursued while a backlog of 1,000 cases waited their turn. In 70% of the cases reviewed by the Innocence Project, claims of innocence could not be supported with DNA, (no biological evidence was available for testing), and therefore had to be rejected. In some states there are no laws preventing the destruction of biological evidence after a jury has reached its verdict, undermining DNA-based appeals by plaintiffs.

The Innocence Project employs the resources of the Cardozo School of Law Legal Clinic, where law students do research and legal writing under the supervision of law professors. So far, their efforts have freed over 30 people across the nation, and Neufeld predicts that thousands of prisoners might be exonerated if only states would grant them the right to have DNA testing done.[16]

It has been Professor Neufeld's experience that in most of the project's cases, prosecutors fight against requests by prisoners to do DNA testing. Barry Scheck echoed that frustration at a meeting of the National Commission on the Future of DNA Evidence, saying that requests by the project to have DNA testing done on biological evidence being held in some state crime labs are often ignored or dismissed out of hand. Worse still, Scheck said, "We encounter every day across this country cases where DNA has exonerated individuals and the court system is extremely reluctant to let them go."[17] In a recent case, Vincent Jenkins was exonerated by DNA evidence for a rape he was convicted of nearly 17 years ago. Mr. Jenkins was given a life sentence for the crime, and despite the fact he has proven his innocence, lawyers from the office of the Erie County District Attorney told a New York Times reporter in September of 1999 that they will continue to oppose efforts by Jenkin's lawyers to have a federal judge rule that he should be freed because his innocence has been established.[18]

Why is this scenario being repeated across the country? Professor Scheck hypothesizes that the reluctance to free innocent prisoners occurs "because people pay a price when these things come out. Even if it's nobody's fault ... it looks like a political embarrassment."[19]

To date, only Illinois and New York have recognized the near impossibility of getting prosecutors to cooperate in the pursuit of justice and have responded by enacting laws giving prisoners the right to postconviction DNA testing. As a result of the laws, both states are freeing wrongfully convicted prisoners at rates that exceed the national average. Scheck claims that because of these statutes, Illinois has seen 14 postconviction exonerations and New York has seen seven, representing nearly one-third of all U.S. prisoners that successfully used DNA to prove their innocence in the last decade.[20] For the sake of justice, both Scheck and Neufeld propose that similar statutes be enacted in other states or by the federal government.

What about the claims of innocence that cannot be supported by biological evidence? A case in point occurred in 1982, when a 24-year-old black engineer named Lenell Geter was arrested in Dallas for an armed robbery. Despite the fact that Geter was on the job at E-Systems at the time the crime happened, he was still arrested, convicted of the crime by an all-white jury and sentenced to life in prison. Geter's co-workers raised some money for his appeal and the NAACP entered the picture. Before long, an outraged media had

131

revealed this travesty of justice: Dallas County District Attorney Henry Wade had been willing to lock Geter away forever, despite the fact that his whereabouts at the time of the robbery were easily verifiable.

It took two years for Geter to see justice, and he was released without apology from the district attorney. Upon his release, Geter expressed concern that there were other people in similar predicaments, without benefit of public support and media scrutiny. "People expect our judicial system to work in a 100% efficiency mode," the engineer said. "I know it doesn't, and I'm a prime example. There are other Lenell Geters out there."[21] Charles Hartford, Geter's supervisor at E-Systems added, "The law enforcement people and the district attorney didn't try to find the truth; they just tried to get a conviction."[22]

Besides the obvious racial element in the Geter case, the ineptitude of police and the callousness of the district attorney were also contributing factors to a wrongful conviction. Mr. Geter's exposure to injustice drove him to explore what could be done to punish those who had harmed him and maybe keep them from harming others. Geter's lawyer, Edwin Sigel of Dallas, describes well the limited recourse available to innocents who have suffered at the hands of malicious or incompetent police and prosecutors. He said, "There is absolute immunity on the part of the district attorney's office. As long as they are dealing in good faith, nothing can be done. As for the police, they have a certain amount of immunity."[23] Pace Law School professor, Benett L. Gershman added, "If a prosecutor withholds evidence, it's not a crime. The fact is that criminal prosecutions of prosecutors for matters relating to their professional responsibilities in American law are virtually unknown, inconceivable, unthinkable."[24] In their treatise on wrongful conviction, Huff and partners attempted to identify the sources and distribution of errors in our criminal justice system. They created a database of 205 cases and what they discovered was that in nearly half those cases of wrongful conviction, eyewitness misidentification played a role. In one out of ten cases, perjury by witnesses or negligence by criminal justice officials were cited as other causes of wrongful conviction. False or coerced confessions surfaced in almost eight percent of the cases studied. Though the Huff study concluded that several causes of wrongful conviction often work simultaneously, the following observation was made:

"If we had to isolate a single 'system dynamic' that pervades large numbers of these cases, we would probably describe it as police and prosecutorial overzealousness: the anxiety to solve a case; the ease with which one having such anxiety is willing to believe, on the slightest evidence of the most negligible nature, that the culprit is at hand; the willingness to use improper, unethical and illegal means to obtain a conviction when one believes that the person at the bar is guilty."[25]

More recently, the issue of witness manipulation is surfacing as a cause of wrongful conviction, especially in alleged crimes involving child abuse. In Massachusetts, the Fells Acres Day School, operated by the Amirault family, was the source of horrific child abuse allegations beginning over 13 years ago. The investigation of allegations, which exploited the suggestibility of children who attended the day-care, resulted in the conviction of three Amirault family members. Though those convictions were eventually overturned, in August of 1999 the Supreme Judicial Court of Massachusetts reinstated the convictions, a decision that upset many people familiar with the case. The <u>Christian Science Monitor</u> noted that it was "the second time in two years the court refused to correct... a prosecution that should never have been brought."[26] Dorothy Rabinowitz, writing in the <u>Wall Street Journal</u>, said that this was "a case built on testimony from children who were bribed and badgered until they said they were abused."[27]

In October of 1999, public pressure saw Cheryl Amirault released from prison through a modification of sentence, from prison time to probation. Given the investment of time and money in convicting the Amiraults, the justice system of Massachusetts was reluctant to admit fault in the matter. In exchange for her freedom, Ms. Amirault had to agree not to oppose the sentence revision, give any television interviews, or pursue further efforts to prove her innocence. So much for courts being fact finding forums. Though Cheryl Amirault's mother was freed before she died, her brother, Gerald, still languishes behind bars.

A similar story was recently repeated in Edenton, North Carolina, where the owner of the Little Rascals Day-Care Center, Robert Kelly, was vindicated in the fall of 1999 after having been convicted of child sexual abuse charges in 1992 and sentenced to 12 consecutive life terms.

On the West Coast, an even more bizarre case is still unfolding, one where 43 people were brought up on child abuse charges in 1994 and 1995 in the small town of Wenatchee, Washington. Prosecutors alleged that groups of Wenatchee citizens gathered once or twice a week for the purpose of sexually abusing scores of children.[28] Two girls, then aged 10 and 12, pointed out most of the 23 homes where these abuses had allegedly happened and named many of the adults who were supposedly involved. These two star witnesses, as it turns out, were living in case detective Robert Perez's home when the allegations were made. The relationship between the girls and the detective resulted in nearly 29,000 counts of sex crimes being brought before the grand jury, including allegations of group sex and even church orgies.

As the incredible stories of abuse unfolded, the Washington Department of Social and Health Services was asked to provide counseling to the victims. After interviewing a 15-year-old who recanted her story of sexual abuse, Social Worker Paul Glassen reported his findings to investigators. Shortly afterwards, police entered Glassen's office and arrested him for witness tampering and several other offenses. Mr. Glassen was fired from his job and his name began showing up on Detective Perez's child molester lists. Glassen fled to Canada to avoid imprisonment and fought the allegations against him from Vancouver, British Columbia. Before he succeeded in clearing his name through civil suits, Glassen had been made a suspect in the molestation of over 50 children.

At this time, Wenatchee prosecutors are fighting against the groundswell of public support that is resulting in the reversals of the convictions they fought so hard to win back in '94 and '95. It is becoming increasingly apparent that prosecutors may have succeeded in ruining the lives of 43 innocent citizens, imprisoning 21 of them, by responding to the community outrage engendered by a flawed investigation. One would think such travesties impossible in this information age, a time when science supposedly reigns over ignorance. Unfortunately for the wrongfully accused, in matters involving children, people tend to be guided by heartfelt passions instead of objective clarity.

The Reverend James McCloskey, Director of Centurion Ministries, another group that works to free innocent prisoners, alludes to public apathy as another cause of wrongful conviction: "I realize I am a voice crying in the wilderness, but I believe that the innocent are convicted far more frequently than the public cares to believe, and far more frequently than those who operate the system dare to believe. An innocent in prison, in my view, is about as rare as a pigeon in the park."[29]

In its 20 year history, Centurion Ministries, an organization operated by volunteers and funded with donations and grants, has freed 20 people from prison. As is the case with all organizations attempting to correct injustice, Centurion Ministries is forced to severely stretch its limited resources. At the start of 2000, there are 14 cases to which they are committed, cases sifted from the thousands of pleas for help they receive from prisoners.

In his experience in freeing the innocent, Reverend McCloskey estimates that 10% of people convicted of serious crimes are innocent. He attributes the epidemic of injustice in part to the work performed by crime lab "experts."

"We see instance after instance where the prosecutor's crime laboratory experts cross the line from science to advocacy. They exaggerate the results of their analysis of hairs, fibers, blood or semen in such a manner that it is absolutely devastating to the defendant. To put the defendants at further disadvantage, the defense attorneys do not educate themselves in the forensic science in question, and therefore conduct a weak cross-examination. Also, in many cases, the defense does not call its own forensic experts, whose testimony in numerous instances could severely damage the state's scientific analysis."[30]

Another source of injustice stems from police officers' willingness to do most anything to obtain a conviction, especially when encouraged overtly or tacitly by prosecutors. "What would surprise and even shock most jury members is the extent to which police officers lie on the stand to reinforce the prosecution and not jeopardize their standing within their own particular law enforcement community," said Reverend McCloskey. "The words of one 25 year veteran senior officer on a northern New Jersey police force still ring in my ears: 'They [the defense] lie, so we [the police] lie. I don't know one of my fellow officers who hasn't lied under oath.'"[31]

Lies are one thing, but as the well publicized incidents of police brutality in New York City indicate, sometimes police get so far out of hand as to become the criminals. One recent case involves Los Angeles' anti-gang CRASH unit, an acronym that stands for Community Resources Against Street Hoodlums. An officer in the employ of the CRASH program was caught stealing cocaine; in exchange for a lighter sentence, he agreed to describe the criminal activities of fellow officers, including the brutal shooting of a handcuffed, unarmed teenager. The revelation of criminal activities of several police officers has resulted in two men being freed from prison with the likelihood that dozens will follow. Jesse Walker, who wrote about the CRASH incident in Reason magazine, asked a valid question regarding police criminality: "Who's supposed to protect us when a militarized police force starts adopting gangster values?"[32]

In researching for this essay, I found hundreds of documented cases where innocent lives had been destroyed by injustice for any number of reasons, some simple and others complicated. Facts show that far too frequently, despite our safeguards, wrongful convictions occur. Ask yourself, in light of the facts presented in this essay, if you too could become a victim of injustice through no fault of your own through any one of several failings in our justice system. To end the national disgrace of wrongful conviction, caring citizens must first agree that the problem exists. Martin Luther King Jr. once said, "Injustice anywhere is a threat to justice everywhere." His wise observation supports the proposition that injustice in a courtroom invariably results in a loss of trust in our judicial institutions. How can we reduce the incidence of injustice by wrongful conviction? What more can we do to protect the integrity of our justice system? Here are some ideas to consider:

1. In view of the inevitable errors in judgment to which humans are subject, abolish the death penalty and replace it with life imprisonment. The possibility of killing even one more innocent citizen should be anathema to a society that prides itself on the equitable distribution of justice. Why deprive ourselves the opportunity to correct errors in judgment?

2. Enact state laws to make it illegal to destroy biological evidence gathered at crime scenes until the value of that evidence is ascertained through DNA testing.

3. Also enact state laws allowing for the testing of biological evidence, at state expense, in cases where such testing could support claims of innocence or establish guilt. These laws should also provide for the education and training of law enforcement personnel regarding DNA testing and the procedures for gathering biological evidence to conduct that testing.

4. Provide police academy recruits with case histories of wrongful conviction along with academic research on the subject. Police who are aware of the incidence and causes of wrongful conviction would be better able to avoid the pitfalls that lead to innocent people being arrested.

5. Modify our adversarial system of justice from one focused on pitched courtroom battles to one focused on the pursuit of truth. Harvard professor, Lloyd Weinreb, offers a starting point:

"Transfer of investigative responsibility from the police to a legally trained judicial officer allows unification of the independent investigations of the prosecution and defense into a single investigation, the outcome of which is a careful conclusion supported by the evidence .... The declared purpose of the investigation should be to find out what happened, not develop a case for either side."[33]

6. Give judges greater latitude to work with juries during trials, allowing for better understanding of evidence by having juror questions and concerns addressed.

7. Provide state courts of appeal with budgets for hiring independent investigators to be used in cases where claims of innocence or accusations of guilt cannot be supported by biological evidence, particularly in cases where eyewitness identification is the sole evidence.

8. The financial constraints of defendants should not limit, in any manner, access to justice. Generously compensate court appointed attorneys to improve the quality of representation for indigents.

9. Protect defendants from the pressure to plea bargain in cases where innocence is supported by evidence or lack of it.

10. Insist on accountability for any player in the judicial system who deviates from the obligation to arrive at justice through the pursuit of truth. If law enforcement officials knowingly alter or fabricate evidence in order to achieve a conviction, they should be removed from their positions of trust. Malicious or incompetent agents of the court should not be protected by state law from civil lawsuits seeking redress for harm caused to innocent citizens.

11. Ban prosecutors from soliciting or accepting testimony from jailhouse informants. Desperate prisoners, hoping for favors or relief, typically make unreliable witnesses.

12. Establish state protocol to assist wrongfully convicted citizens with reintegration into free society. Those protocol should also address the issue of fair compensation for the losses and suffering caused by injustice.

13. Establish more law school legal clinics and enlist them to provide legal assistance to prisoners filing appeals. The success of legal clinics in rooting out truth and pursuing justice is so indisputable as to merit the financial support of state and federal governments.

14. Perhaps fewer innocents would fall victim to wrongful conviction if we demanded that our burgeoning prison-industrial complex measure its success, not by the growth of its inmate population, but rather by its decline.

In closing, I would like to pass along messages from two men who survived the ordeal of wrongful conviction. In a telephone interview, Kerry Max Cook explained that he made it through 17 years on death row in Texas because of his faith in a higher power. But it was the knowledge of his innocence that gave him the courage to engage the state in legal battle on numerous occasions, succeeding in overturning his case not once, but three times, before he was finally freed.

In a recent television interview, Reuben "Hurricane" Carter, who survived 19 years in the New Jersey prison system, convicted of a triple murder he never committed, encourages people who suffer from the ignoble fate of wrongful conviction to fight the injustice they endure by having the fortitude to dare to dream. His experience fighting injustice from a prison cell also yielded a caveat: "The one thing I learned in prison is that bitterness consumes the vessel that contains it."

May the courage, wisdom and success of all people who have succeeded in their battles to correct injustice inspire those whose fights are still young.

RESOURCES

Center on Wrongful Conviction, 357 East Chicago Avenue, Chicago, IL 60611, (312)503-8576
A collaboration between Medill Journalism School and Northwestern University Legal Clinic. The legal clinic assists prisoners whose cases withstand the scrutiny of the journalism school.

Centurion Ministries, 32 Nassau Street, Princeton, NJ 08543, (609)921-0334
Assists prisoners, especially those with long sentences or on death row, through the application of conventional investigative techniques.

Innocence Project, Cardozo School of Law, 55 Fifth Avenue, New York, NY 10003, (212)790-0354
Works with prisoners in advancing DNA issues.

Association of the Wrongly Convicted, 155 Delaware Avenue, Toronto, Canada M6H 2T2,

FOOTNOTES

1. Dallas Observer Online, July 15, 1999.
http://www.dallasobserver.com/issues/1999-07-15/feature-5.html
2. Ibid.
3. Ibid.
4. Ibid.
5. Ibid.
6. "Miscarriages of Justice in Potentially Capital Cases," 40 Stanford Law Review, pp. 23, 36.
7. "Protecting the Innocent: A Response to the Bedau-Radelet Study," 41 Stanford Law Review, p. 121.
8. Martin Yant, Presumed Guilty: When Innocent People Are Wrongly Convicted, (New York: Prometheus Books, 1991), p. 207.
9. Ibid.
10. "DNA Tests Are Freeing Scores of Prison Inmates," New York Times, April 19, 1999.
11. C.R. Huff et. al., Convicted But Innocent: Wrongful Conviction and Public Policy, (California: Sage Publications, 1993), p.50.
12. "Unlocking the Cells," Reason, January 2000, p.50.
13. Ibid.
14. National Institute of Justice Report, Postconviction DNA Testing Recommendations for Handling Requests, September 1999, p. iii.
15. "Unlocking the Cells," Reason, January 2000, p.51.
16. Ibid.

17. National Commission on the Future of DNA Evidence, Meeting VI Proceedings, p.3 (of on-line transcript). http://www.ojp.usdoj.gov/nij/dnamtgtrans6/trans-c.html
18. "How Many Innocent Prisoners?" New York Times, July 18, 1999.
19. National Commission on the Future of DNA Evidence, Meeting VI Proceedings, p.13 (of on-line transcript). http://www.ojp.usdoj.gov/nij,/dnamtgtrans6/trans-c.html
20. Ibid., p.7.
21. Martin Yant, Presumed Guilty: When Innocent People Are Wrongfully Convicted (New York: Prometheus Books, 1991) pp.18,19.
22. Ibid, p.19.
23. "Innocents in Jail," ABA LawScope, June 1984, pp.34,35.
24. "The Wrong Man," The Atlantic Monthly, November 1999, p.74.
25. C.R. Huff et. al., Convicted But Innocent: Wrongful Conviction and Public Policy (California: Sage Publications, 1993), p.64.
26. Dorothy Rabinowitz, "The Pursuit of Justice," Wall Street Journal, October 7, 1999
27. Ibid.
28. "Reckoning in Wenatchee," Wall Street Journal, Sept. 21, 1999.
29. Martin Yant, Presumed Guilty: When Innocent People Are Wrongfully Convicted (New York: Prometheus Books, 1991) Prologue.
30. Ibid, p.68.
31. Ibid, p.128.
32. "Gangsta Cops," Reason, January 2000, p.13.
33. Martin Yant, Presumed Guilty: When Innocent People AreWrongfully Convicted (New York: Prometheus Books, 1991) p.219.

REFERENCE LIST

1.Bailey, Ronald, "Unlocking the Cells," Reason, January 2000, pp. 50-51
2.Bedau, Adam & Radelet, Michael, "Miscarriage of Justice in Potentially Capital Cases," Stanford Law Review, 1987 (Vol. 40), pp. 21-81
3.Berlow, Alan, "The Wrong Man," The Atlantic Monthly, November 1999, pp. 66-91
4.Dallas Observer Online Features, July 15, 1999
http://www.dallasobserver.com/issues/1999-07-15/features-5.html
5.Dedman, Bill, "DNA Tests Are Freeing Scores of Inmates, "New York Times, April 19, 1999
6.Herbert, Bob, "How Many Innocent Prisoners," New York Times, July 18, 1999
7.Howlett, Debbie, "National Spotlight on Wrongful Convictions," The Echo, January/February/ March, 1999
8.Huff, C.R. et al., Convicted But Innocent: Wrongful Conviction and Public Policy, California: Sage Publications, 1992
9.Markham, Stephen & Cassell, Paul, "Protecting the Innocent: A Response to the Bedau-Radelt Study," November 1988, pp. 121-161
10.National Commission on the Future of DNA Evidence Meeting VI Proceedings
http//www.pbj.usdoj.gov/nij/dnamtgtrans6/trans-c.html
11.Quade, Vicki, "Innocents in Jail," LawScope, June 1984, pp. 34-35
12.Rabinowitz, Dorothy,"The Pursuit of Justice, Continued," Wall Street Journal, October 7, 1999
13.Rabinowitz, Dorothy, "Cheryl Amirault is Freed," Wall Street Journal, October 22, 1999
14.Rabinowitz, Dorothy, "Reckoning in Wenatchee," Wall Street Journal, September 21, 1999
15.Walker, Jesse, "Gangsta Cops," Reason, January 2000, p. 13
16.Yant, Martin, Presumed Guilty: When Innocent People Are Wrongly Convicted, New York: Prometheus Books, 1991

Dennis J. Dechaine *is serving a life sentence at the Maine State Prison. He is a client of The Innocence Project.*

OUT OF THE BLACK AND INTO THE BLUE

Arthur DeTullio

And so the day had finally arrived. After ten years, four months and 16 days, I was now going to be able to trade in my identity as "convict" for the slightly less stigmatic label of "ex-con."

I hardly slept the night before. All night I paced the confines of the cell or lay awake staring at the ceiling and thinking about freedom. Freedom. There was an exhilaration in the thought, along with a strong dose of fear. It seemed slightly contradictory to be afraid of being free. For over a decade, I had been awaiting this moment with every waking breath. Now that the moment was upon me, I felt the fear one feels when entering into a new, and possibly dangerous, territory.

I was not being released from the state prison; I had spent the last 30 days of my incarceration housed in the Plymouth County House of Correction. My state sentence had been up a month before. The House time was for a charge I had received ten years earlier, while still a prisoner at the Bridgewater State Hospital. I had assaulted a guard there by spitting in his face, and the court had refused to run the time concurrent with my state sentence.

The last 30 days had been both a form of decompression and a revelation as to what awaited me in the world. Many things had changed in the past decade. My House stay had been my first real encounter with the phenomenon known as the crack addict, for one thing. When I entered Walpole, crack had just begun to appear on the street. It hadn't reached the epidemic proportions that it would over the last decade. By the time most of these people had hit Walpole, they had been off the streets for at least a few months awaiting sentencing in the county jail. By the time I saw them, they had been all cleaned up. Here, they were fresh from the streets, reeking and filthy and slightly insane from detoxification.

This was also the first time in many years that I had been with anyone who had recently been free. I was meeting people who, only hours earlier, had been walking the streets. I was watching prisoners working the telephones, trying like mad to come up with bail money to get released. I was listening to conversations that were alien to my ears. I heard men bitching and complaining about sentences of 30 days, 60 days, four months -- time I could not even begin to fathom.

And I was an alien to them, too. They avoided me for the most part. Word had circulated throughout the block that I was wrapping up the tail end of over ten years on the inside and I was viewed as some sort of bizarre oddity, all of which was fine with me. I had nothing to say to these men. We didn't even speak the same language.

I continued to pace the length of the cell block, eyes watching the clock like a prowling cat watches the sparrow. Dawn was coming to pick me up. I was so excited by the prospect of spending my first day of freedom with her. All those years of waiting, of wanting, of hoping were now coming to reality. The fact that Dawn was picking me up worked to temper what fear I had of being released. At least I knew that, no matter what confronted me today, she would be there beside me to help and guide me through it. And finally the moment I had been awaiting for over a decade. The phone on the guard desk rang and I saw him looking over at me. This was it.

"DeTullio, pack it up. You're outta here."

Sweet words. Words like water on the lips of a man dying from thirst.

The property officer dressed me out in my street clothes and all that remained was to sign my release papers. I sat in a plastic chair in the booking area waiting for the guards to process me out, and through the tall glass windows that looked out on the visiting lobby, I saw Dawn come in. Only the width of the shatter-proof glass separated us and we were all smiles and anticipation.

The June morning was ripe with the promise of a hot summer day as Dawn and I strolled the length of the parking lot to her car -- so many emotions running rampant in my mind. I was free. Like Lazurus, I too had just risen from the dead. For the first time in longer than my body could recall, I was on the other side of the wall and no chains or manacles weighed down my limbs or my soul. Freedom. I wanted to dance crazy on the asphalt, shout out my excitement and my joy, grab Dawn up in my arms and devour her lips with my mouth. I was free.

So excited were we by my release that Dawn and I drove out of the parking lot more concerned with each other than with where we were going. We were supposed to be heading to Maine, home for us both. As we drove along, enjoying the closeness, the conversation, the actual ability to talk, touch, smile and laugh with no guards or cameras or restrictions put upon us, we paid little attention to direction.

"Where's Fall River?" asked Dawn, about a half-hour into our drive.

"It's down on the Rhode Island border," I answered. "Why?"

"Because we just entered it, according to that sign," she said.

Rather than turning north from the parking lot, we had driven south, going about 60 miles round trip out of our way.

"Well," I laughed, "looks like we're gonna see Fall River." And that is what we did. We laughed and took a ride around the ocean in Fall River, Massachusetts.

How quickly sunlight can turn to darkness. How short the time between bliss and ruin. No Oracle I, but had I the power of prophecy, I would have seen the future in the first act of that day. In less than nine months, I would be so different from that happy, laughing person. In less than nine months, I would not laugh about something so innocent, something so humorous. In that time, I would become cold, hard, mean spirited and cruel. Such an error then would lead to a tantrum, a rage, an abusive verbal assault or a cold silent contempt.

It wasn't just the car that was headed in a wrong direction that morning, it was also me. My destination was where I had always wanted to be, but my journey would be one of anger, denial and a convict's mentality of secrets, arrogance and spreading the pain.

But for the day, life had a golden hue I had rarely, if ever, basked in before. It wasn't without its moments of trepidation and anxiety, however. Driving through Boston was an assault upon my senses. The stench of exhaust fumes was a forgotten experience as we languished in the morass of slowly moving traffic, nose and stomach pounded by the sickening smells. But the brightness of the colors surrounding me were a pleasant distraction from the odorous attack upon my stomach. Never before had blue seemed so cool or red so vibrant. Splashes of orange and eruptions of green, pink and purple leaped out in glowing bursts. The whole spectrum of the color scale shimmered and exploded before my eyes. Prison, in its harshest reality, is the absence of all beauty and softness. Freedom was a feast to my sensory starved soul.

Once out on the open highway, the rest of the ride back to Maine was a joyous experience. Everything felt brand new, like sitting in the front seat of a car, playing the radio, having actual folding paper money in my pocket, being beside Dawn. The first real jolt upon my senses, my wake-up call to reality, had yet to occur. It was soon in coming, however. We arrived in Portsmouth, New Hampshire, and Dawn said she had an errand to run before it got too late. I wanted to purchase a "Walkman" cassette player for my running, so I suggested that she drop me off at the appliance store, run her errand and pick me up downtown in the local park.

"How you going to get to the park?" she asked.

"Don't worry, I'll catch a cab and meet you there in about an hour."

"Okay, as long as you think you're gonna be all right."

"Don't worry, I'll be fine."

She dropped me in the parking lot of a large chain appliance store and drove off. The electronic doors opened smoothly and silently as I approached, and I stepped inside. The first thing to assault my sensibilities was a solid wall of television sets, row upon row of televisions, all turned on, all blazing in color and motion. I turned my head left and right, momentarily dazed, and there on one of the televisions was me!

I looked again. A camcorder, a device I was only vaguely familiar with, stood on a tripod near the door projecting the image of anyone entering the store upon a large screen television set right in the middle of the aisle.

Panic came in waves of adrenaline, surging through my nervous system and causing my heart to race. Everywhere around me people jostled and moved, color blurred in torrents of motion. My chest grew tight with anxiety, making it hard to breath. I was positive that everyone in there was staring at me, that they all knew I had just been released from prison. My irrational mind was whirling and I had to get out of that store.

I turned and rushed through the doors, feeling the panic lessen just in the act of getting outside. I stood in the parking lot, gulping air and attempting to compose myself. After a moment, I felt the adrenaline receding. My heart beat returned to normal and I prepared myself to try again. I reentered the store, emotionally prepared for the psychic assault upon my senses. This time it was different; I was ready and I quickly overcame the panic before it had the chance to rise. I walked over to the television where my image was again on the screen and watched as I was replaced by the next person entering the store. Seeing someone else's face on the television calmed whatever was left of my paranoia. I was not a victim of Big Brother, but rather just an unwitting participant in a store display. It was then that I saw the camcorder on its tripod and figured out what was going on. Technology had made some interesting advances in the past 10 years.

Actually purchasing the cassette player that I wanted turned out to be easier than I expected. There was a moment of brief surrealism as I actually paid for it with real money from my pocket. I stood in the check-out line for a moment, expecting the clerk to hand me my commissary card to sign. The look on his face as he waited on me was a reminder that I could carry my own money now. I paid the price and left the store. I wasn't quite through with my cultural reentry shock yet, though. There were still a few more surprises awaiting me.

After leaving the store, my new "Walkman" and a new tape in hand, I began looking for a pay phone to call a cab. I found one in the parking lot of a grocery store across the street. The first thing I noticed was the absence of a phone book. No problem, just call the operator and ask for Information. I put in my dime and pressed zero. Nothing. I hung up the phone and tried again. Still nothing. It was then that I saw the price of a phone call had gone to a quarter. Still no problem. I pulled a quarter from my pocket and repeated the process. The next thing I knew, I was listening to a long recording telling me what digit to press for what service I was requesting. I stood there for about five minutes, pressing buttons and getting nowhere, and the frustration was mounting to the point that I began cursing the phone.

"Sonofabitch, where the Christ's the goddamn Information operator?" I started to mutter.

I pressed a few more buttons and still could get no human on the line.

"What the fuck's going on here?" I barked, louder now. "How the fuck do I get Information?"

It was then that I looked around and noticed a few people on the sidewalk staring at me. I could feel the paranoia rising again along with my convict mentality. I wanted to snarl at them, "What the fuck you looking at?" Instead I tried the phone one more time. Again that infuriating recording.

Finally, an older man who had been watching me growing more and more frustrated walked over and asked me what the problem was.

"What's the matter, son? You look like you're about to break the phone off the wall."

"I can't figure out how to get Information. All I wanna do is call a cab and all I keep getting is this goddamn recording and it won't tell me what I need to do!"

He was looking at me like I had just grown another head right in front of him, and held out his hand for the receiver.

"Here, let me," he said.

A few seconds later he looked at me and asked me what cab company I wanted. Another decision. I didn't have a clue what to ask for.

"I dunno," I said. "Anyone, I guess."

He listened for a moment, hung up the phone, put another quarter in the slot and dialed.

"There you go, " he said, handing me the phone.

A few rings later and I had finally called my cab. As I hung up the phone, I thanked the man for his help.

"Been away for a while?" he asked.

"Yeah, you could say that."

The park was a green oasis after the storm of paranoia and anxiety I had just sailed. I walked around for a bit, enjoying the newness of it all. So many sensations I had missed for so long I had forgotten I even missed them. The smells were intoxicating. I stood in the center of the park and inhaled through my nose. I could detect the scent of flowers, the lingering aroma of feminine perfume, the smell of cooking meat from the pushcart vendors surrounding the park, the sharp brine of sea water from the river. The air was a calliope of fragrances playing a melodious symphony for my long deprived nose.

And trees. For 10 years, I had seen only the tops of trees over the height of the wall. I walked around touching the trees, running my hand along their trunks, feeling the rough texture of bark on some, the smooth velvety surface of others. There was a foreign sensuality in the action, a weird tender sexiness to my caress.

A fountain gurgled in the center of the park, water spouting out of the top and spilling down through layers of little pools. I stood beside it watching how the sunlight sparkled off of the rippling little waves, listening to the sound of the water mingling with the laughter of children and the faint murmur of conversations.

I was sitting peacefully on a stone bench listening to my new cassette player when I saw Dawn entering the park.

"How'd everything go?" she asked.

I laughed, telling her the story of the store and the phone. Now it was time to finish the drive and go to my father's house in Maine where I was going to be living.

The old neighborhood had changed over the years, so many new homes where there used to be just empty field. We drove past the house where I grew up. My father still owned it, but he no longer lived there. After everyone had grown and moved out, it had become just too big for my mother and him alone, so they had moved into the new house, built when I had been in prison. My mother had died in February, only four short months before my release. It felt strange to enter the house, knowing that I would not be seeing my mother sitting in her customary place at the kitchen table.

The next two weeks were filled with discovery and activity. There were graves I had to visit that set off echoes in my soul that only served to remind me of just how long I was away. Everywhere I turned there was some new toy or device to amaze and bewilder. Cell phones and compact disks were fantastic new experiences. Television now required special magazines and devices to keep up with the new multitude of channels and special access programming. Finding a show was as confusing as algebra. Telephones were infuriating adventures with real live operators seemingly banished forever to be replaced by confounding recordings that took you through a long maze of messages and choices, but never, it seemed, where you actually wanted to go.

I spent every day with Dawn, rediscovering the simple fact that I truly loved this woman more than I could ever love any other woman in my life. We took picnic lunches, went for drives, went shopping, ate at restaurants, walked the beach, everything except make love. It would be two whole weeks before she was ready for that.

Making love. Not sex, not fucking, but making love. I had dreamt of the moment, of course, had lived for the moment, in fact. I was bursting with desire, but, for the first time in my life, I was willing to delay my needs and passions. I had made myself a promise while still in prison that the first time I made love to a woman it would be a meaningful experience, not simply a satisfaction of lust. It was meant to be Dawn, of this I was sure, and so I was willing to wait.

It was well worth the wait.

Within less then a month's time, I was living with Dawn. My next major task was to find a job. I accomplished this much more easily than I expected. Everywhere I seemed to turn, life was unfolding for me in wonderful and amazing ways. People and family were showing support and lending aid in ways I never expected. I was invited to appear on a local cable television show in Cambridge, Massachusetts, to talk about my prison experiences. I was given aid and support in my writing endeavors. I was seeking visitation rights with my son, and already seeing my daughter. There was only one way to improve the quality of my life. Dawn and I decided to get married.

It was as gorgeous a summer day as could be hoped for. A Sunday, the fourth day of August, 1996. We were married on my father's second floor deck with a beautiful ocean view and our families in attendance. The only imperfection of the day for me was the noticeable absence of my mother and nephew, both dead, and my two children.

My life was turning out better than I ever dared to dream. My nights were filled with love and romance with my wife and the hot summer days seemed to stretch on endlessly. Naked romps in the swimming pool with Dawn, candlelight dinners, even trips to the grocery store were adventures. But the Beast was not dead, merely sleeping.

I didn't drink for almost the first five months of my freedom. I didn't smoke and even kept up with my running and writing for a time. But everything inside me was still there, all that suppressed rage from years and years of confinement and isolation, all the paranoia, the secretiveness, the hatred, the violence, the alcoholism, the addictions. I wasn't tending to my soul. I knew in my heart that I needed to address these issues, but my arrogance over-rode my understanding.

Prison steals so much. It twists and warps in ways you are not even aware of. If you are the least bit twisted inside to begin with, have any real anger or depression or hate inside you at all, the prison experience will feed these traits and defects, allowing them to fester and grow within like a cancerous tumor.

It began with little things, like it so often does. The peace and the calm I possessed upon my release was eroding a little more each day. Small incidents would reverberate inside, setting off larger issues and releasing the repressed anger. The martyr complex I had refined so well over the years in prison was turning each small conflict into major conspiracies against me. It was easier to focus the blame elsewhere and spread around my pain than to actually take responsibility for me. Having spent the greatest portion of my life running as fast as I could and dealing with any type of pain or problem by drowning it in booze and drugs, I was in no position to cope with the demons when they made their reappearance in my life. I began to punish those I loved the most and who loved me the most, almost as if I were penalizing them for being so foolish as to love me in the first place. The beginning of the end for me was when I finally picked up the alcohol again -- gasoline in the blast furnace of my rage.

Not long after I began to drink, I also started smoking cigarettes once more. For three years I had gone without a cigarette and was extremely proud of this accomplishment. When I picked them up again, I decided to blame Dawn rather than taking responsibility and admitting the role of the alcohol. Soon after, I started playing with drugs again. In no time, I blew up to over 200 pounds. I rarely, if ever, sat down to write. Self-loathing was a constant companion and the worse I felt, the more I took my pain out on my wife and my family.

The true end began with a night of drunken insanity. Before the night was over, I had been arrested for assaulting my wife and one other person.

I still didn't get it. I still lived in a world shaded with denial, arrogance, self-righteousness and self-pity. I was still operating with a convict mentality. Drunk, I had physically hit my wife, the one woman who I was supposed to never hurt, either bodily or emotionally, and still I was drinking almost everyday. Rather than admit to my alcoholism, I was sliding deeper and deeper into a world of unreality. I was charged with two counts of assault, facing the possibility of going back inside, yet I was only looking at ways to get away with it, how to get out of it. So immersed was I in my denial, I never even told Dawn I was sorry.

And so, after 21 months of freedom, I returned to jail once again. The deal was for one year with six months suspended and four months to actually serve after good-time deductions. And the court agreed to work release so I wouldn't lose my job.

My release came on the first day of July, 1998. On July 2, Dawn left me. She announced over dinner in a Chinese restaurant that she wanted a divorce. Who could blame her? For almost two years she had given me everything and I had only wanted more and more.

It was like the world ceased to spin for me. Never had I felt so much pain, so much torment. I spent the next week or so walking and driving around in a haze of tears, anger and remorse. Alcohol was my constant companion and my only solace. One night, after a bitter fight at what used to be our home, my wife walked out and slammed the door in my face. I drove around in a semi-drunken fog, contemplating my own death.

I was a broken man. Prison couldn't break me; I was too tough for that. The hole couldn't break me, the street couldn't, not drink nor drugs. Sixteen years inside the Hate Factories hadn't been able to tear me down. But to lose Dawn and to know, to have no doubts whatsoever, that it was entirely my own fault, is what finally brought me to the bottom. I was defeated.

I might well have died at this point and, in fact, had very little desire left to live. My saving grace, however, was still my wife. Despite everything, she still cared. She witnessed my deterioration and refused to allow me to destroy myself. Following a car wreck in which I totaled my vehicle, she convinced me to seek help. I entered rehab, sought out a counselor and for the first time in my life talked to professionals in the psychiatric field who were truly interested in helping me rather than just being tools for various prison administrations.

It came as a revelation to me when I was diagnosed with severe clinical depression. I was told that I had probably suffered with this for most of my life, so my alcoholism and my drug addictions were merely symptoms of a much larger mental illness that I never even knew I had! I began taking medications that allowed me, for the very first time, to deal with reality on reality's terms.

It was also at this time that I sought out a fellowship of other people who suffered from the same afflictions and obsessions as my own. By following their suggestions and living my life along established and proven principles, I began to see life in an entirely new light. For perhaps the first time ever, I was forced to deal honestly and soberly with myself, my problems and my solutions.

Dawn and I are still separated. We share three wonderful grandchildren, with a fourth on the way, and we now communicate on a level of honesty that we, or at least I, have not know since we first became lovers some 21 years ago.

Life is not without its distractions, problems and frustrations. Life, by definition, is hard. But I now have friends in my life who are there for me, who support my efforts at living clean and sober, and who truly care about my welfare. I am learning, slowly, that the true expression of love is in service to others and in a gentle kindness to myself. I can love no one until I can love myself.

All around me, I see the devastation wrought by alcoholism and drug addiction and I witness a system that deals with these tragedies by constructing more and more prisons while spending for treatment programs are slashed to the bone and programs for rehabilitation in the prisons are abandoned in favor of longer and harsher incarcerations. A person walking out of prison today is thrown into a sink or swim environment and the system refuses to even supply the most basic of life preservers.

I was extremely fortunate to have the support system I had when I was released and even that wasn't enough. Without real intervention measures while behind the wall, the average ex-con is a walking disaster just waiting to happen. Had there been real psychiatric services available to me as far back as my first major incarceration, my clinical depression might have been discovered at a much younger age. This would not only have spared me all those years inside the Hate Factory, it would also have spared society all the carnage I wrought over the course of a lifetime.

I am not unique. Having spent three-quarters of my adult life in prison, I have an awareness of its reality. In my opinion, at least 70-80% of the men I met during my incarcerations suffered from various addictions and mental illnesses. Yet the system refuses to acknowledge this, preferring to place incarceration on a moral platform rather than a medical one. It is true that I met men in prison that I would not want to meet anywhere else except prison, but they are the exception, not the rule.

Rehabilitation works. I am, almost despite myself, proof of this simple fact. Education works. Treatment works. Intervention in the juvenile facilities works, if done right. So, given the facts, why does the spending for new prisons go on at a rate almost 10 times that for new schools? Because prison is an industry and a major growth industry at that. Unlike most major industries, however, prison exists at the expense of the public coffers. And the public's investment is not being served. No board of stockholders would ever allow an industry to continue to function if it operated like prison -- turning out defective products at a rate of 70-80%. Yet the prison industry does just that. It takes the raw material of the young convict and twists and warps it into a walking repository of paranoia, hatred and rage. Rage is not a jacket one can remove at the prison gate upon release. It is a dark and often invisible garment you will wear out into the world. And woe to the world when the day finally arrives when this jacket grows so tight that you must explode in a fit of violence to give yourself some space just to breathe.

The truest reality of the prison experience is that it takes men and women who have done wrong, often times very grievous wrongs, and punishes them to the point where they cannot see their own culpability. They became like children, so abused by their surrogate parents that they can only see themselves as victims rather than taking responsibility for their actions.

So what is the answer? And is there even one at all? I have to believe that there is, although I profess no great wisdom towards its finding. I do, however, have a total of 16 years inside the Belly of the Beast to draw from while seeking a solution. This much I do know: in order for society to be truly served by the incarceration experience, fundamental changes need to be made in the process. Educational and vocational programs need to be expanded, not cut, with some form of job placement services available to the ex-convict upon release. Many men and women return to a life of crime because all other doors appear to be closed. You cannot expect a person to live on the street and starve just to remain out of prison. Likewise, some form of affordable housing needs to exist for those with no place else to go. Perhaps most importantly, psychiatric services must exist to address the post-traumatic excesses of prison. These services should begin while the person is still in custody, but in order for them to have any success rate at all, they must exist as independent bodies not governed by the prison administration. A prisoner must know that his or her sessions will remain private, not be made available to the prison administration as tools to punish or reward at a later date.

These things I suggest are not perfect in and of themselves, nor will they be cheap to implement. But given the cost of incarceration and the social costs of crime and violence, they are extremely affordable alternatives! They need to exist as safety nets, not to support but to guide and nurture the ex-offender in the painful process of reintegration.

In closing, I can only address this reminder to those who scream for the death penalty and a "lock 'em up and throw away the key" approach to prison. I would ask that they remember the words of a famous convict who was executed by the state for his "crimes." His name was Jesus and he said:

"Let he among you who is without sin cast the first stone."

Arthur DeTullio was born in Connecticut and grew up on the coast of Maine. To deal with childhood isolation and trauma, he began drinking and drugging as an adolescent, his criminal career blossoming during his teen years. He is 42 years old and has spent 16 of the past 24 years incarcerated in a number of different state prisons. In 1992, while serving 10-15 years in the Massachusetts State Prison at Walpole, Arthur earned his B.A. in literature from Boston University. He was involved in numerous writing projects during this period, including helping to found the critically acclaimed criminal justice magazine, Odyssey. Arthur was released from Walpole in 1996 and now lives in the great state of Maine where he continues to write, (even now seeking a publisher for his collection of short stories, The Other Side of the Wall.) He enjoys his children and grandchildren and continues to dream of one day reuniting with his ex-wife, Dawn.

RELEVANCE: A MESSAGE FROM THE ARTIST

Matthew Matteo

The courtroom was just as it had been years ago. Nothing had changed -- same wood paneling, high ceilings, red carpeting and chapel atmosphere. All the bad memories I'd managed to repress came flooding back. I'd been here before and knew well the stress of being sentenced.

Everyone stood as the Judge came into the courtroom, black robe flowing; he glided to his seat and began arranging his papers. The Assistant District Attorney, confident and smiling, spoke to a suited colleague and opened his leather briefcase. From within, he produced a heavy file with my name scrawled on it in big letters. That really struck me. This hearing could rewrite the rest of my life.

I had little cause for optimism. After all, the Judge wasn't obligated to alter my sentence and, regrettably, my crimes had been violent. I thought about what I did have going for me. Nine years free of any trouble, no small feat in prison, with only two misconducts, both for minor "write ups" which resulted in warnings. I'd been assigned initially to medium security SCI Rockview and was later transferred to a minimum security facility -- heading in the right direction. However, the philosophy in Pennsylvania is to first treat those inmates who are scheduled for release. As a result, years from eligibility, I had had no rehabilitation or programming in over nine years of prison, nothing accomplished in therapy for my lawyer to work with. Altering my sentence had to come from some evidence of positive change, so I had photocopied a collection of my many published paintings, illustrations and awards I'd won in recent years. I submitted this to my lawyer with a hope and a prayer that this would prove my reform.

My name and case number were announced. With that, my lawyer got up and strode to the podium while I shuffled, ankles shackled, to meet him. Introductions were made and the Judge explained the purpose of the hearing with a noticeable lack of enthusiasm. Nothing was asked of me as the prosecutor established the legitimacy of my lengthy sentence and referred to a wealth of documents. My lawyer countered those claims while the Judge rocked in his chair. Having no role in the hearing, it was as if I were listening to someone else's fate being decided.

Interrupting the illusion, my lawyer turned and asked if I'd tell the court of the success and awards I'd earned in prison. Disoriented by the request to speak on my own behalf for the first time, I asked in a low tone how this, my art, was relevant. His answer was a blank stare. I gathered he didn't know either. It wasn't organized or well thought out, but the words came; I exhausted every memory of my paintings appearing in different journals, of my cartoons published in Louisiana, Minnesota, Michigan, of the calendars and greeting cards, the murals..... I went on and on, hoping this would reflect more of who I am than my thick file. When I couldn't think of anything else, I stood and waited for the unknown. Silence. The judge appeared to be considering what I'd said. He paused, shuffled through his papers and gazed thoughtfully out the window. Then he asked, "And how is this relevant?" I was speechless. This was the same question I'd asked my lawyer only minutes before. Unable to provide an answer, my hopes sank.

That question has echoed in my mind ever since. From the carpeted courtroom to the cold County Jail to the Sheriff's cruiser back to my cell in state prison, I asked myself, "How is this relevant?"

I grew up drawing on everything. In elementary school, kids watched as I brought to life creatures and space aliens in rockets. My projects were displayed in the administration building as examples of student creativity, and my mother complained that I never brought anything home. In high school, I doodled through classes, impressed art teachers and found notoriety through hanging controversial posters.

After graduation, I enrolled at a nearby University where I planned to develop my artistic abilities. However, the freedom, fantastic friends, fraternity parties and dormitory living, the whole college experience intoxicated me. Overconfident and irresponsible, I studied just enough to get through my freshman year. As a sophomore, I began skipping classes, drinking excessively, trading texts for beer money, doing drugs and failing miserably.

The more I failed, the more I invested in addictions, destroying my inhibitions and empathy. So far behind I'd never graduate, I chose a shortcut -- cheating, stealing and lies. The shortcuts led me forever in circles until I was hopelessly lost. Facing my own self-destruction was unbearable; convinced I was powerless, inadequate and worthless, nothing mattered anymore.

The culmination of my failure arrived with a November, 1990 arrest which led to a lengthy prison term. At 22, I'd self-destructed and left a wake of victims behind me. The nightmare wasn't going to end tomorrow or the next day and the blame was mine. Foreseeing years of prison and living among criminals, I wanted to give up. I looked at the others and said, "I'm not as bad as him," or "I didn't do what he did," to feel better. I was minimizing and drawing attention away from what I'd done. But most of those around me hadn't done things worse than me. Was I one of the worst? Shock came in realizing I belonged here. I learned the impact of what I'd done and was forced to look at reality every morning as my cell door unlocked.

The days were numbingly long. When I tired of reading or writing letters, I looked for a pen and drew. Something clicked. I'd destroyed my life and all I knew, but with my ten cent pen, I had returned to the kid I was years and years ago. I'd started over. I could speak volumes about loneliness, frustration and the hope inside me.

For almost a decade, I've painted, drawn, cartooned and illustrated from inside state prison. Dull hours have become precious while the sound of crashing weights, conversation, televisions and card games hum unnoticed around me. By building upon the one positive thing I have left, I've reinvented myself and feel good again. My work has grown and developed and taken on a direction of its own, and so have I. My illustrations and paintings have matured and led to publication and awards and from them I have found empowerment, a voice, confidence and self worth.

Prison has been a crushing adversary, but through it I've realized the best within myself. One door has closed and another opened. I'm inspired and moved by the acceptance I receive from something that's inherently me. I'm at peace with myself and those around me. Erased is the likelihood that I would hurt anyone again through crime.

Your Honor, this is why I feel my accomplishments in art are, in fact, relevant.

Editor's Note

In preparing this manuscript for production, I proudly showed off Matt's artwork to friends and was struck by the variety of interpretations for many of the pieces. A few, of course, were drawn to illustrate specific moments from specific essays and some reflect general prison scenes. But there are those that draw very different responses from different people, an indication, I believe, of the skill of the artist. I very much like the idea that individual readers of <u>Frontiers of Justice</u> can discover a variety of meanings in Matt's pictures; this is why we did not try to title them.

The fellow on the phone (page 93) -- is he a drug dealer, a man on the run with arrest and prison walls closing in? Or has he just been released and is not yet able to move beyond the effects of institutionalization? One friend felt he was still in prison,and phone calls to the outside helped give him a sense of freedom. The inmate drawing in his cell (page 23) -- is he slowly unraveling from his years in prison? Or does his art/writing allow him some escape from his imprisonment? Maybe he is telling us that prison diminishes a man, diminishes us all.

The last picture in the book (page 170) drew strong reactions from everyone. It is the only piece without an obvious prison theme; I initially wondered if I should even include it. Has the woman been in prison and, as is true for so many after release, finds herself with nowhere to go? Is she homeless, without resources, a situation that is too often one step on the road to crime and imprisonment? I think that Russell, whose essay opens this book, provided the best interpretation. On a recent visit, I described this picture to him. He thought for a moment, then presented a title which may well represent every picture, every essay and every poem: "It's a lonely road."

J.Z.

Matthew Matteo is a Pennsylvania prisoner serving a 12½ to 35 year sentence. Born in 1968, he grew up in Derry and later attended nearby Indiana University of Pennsylvania, pursuing a BFA in art. An arrest in 1990 for a series of assaults ended his studies and much more. He's managed to remain positive through publication successes in painting and illustration. Matt's work has been featured in calendars, magazines, books, newsletters, on greeting cards, the internet and in his own pointed prison cartoon series. He continues bettering himself and his art, working towards a brighter future despite a seemingly infinite prison term.

Conclusion: The Right to Live

Scott Antworth

"Prison is where you promise yourself the right to live." Jack Kerouac

"Deer," my father said, stabbing a finger out across the back field to a stand of trees a hundred yards distant. I've always marveled at his woodsman's eye. Not once in my life have I been able to spot the deer, the moose or the fox before him. It was dusk and I was 10 hours into a 12-hour furlough home from the prison farm where I now live. I was out back, sneaking a cigarette with my dad. We watched as the first and then the second wary does slipped from the treeline and into the field, followed by a third, a fourth and finally their buck. My heart was racing. Even in Maine such moments are rare and leave a certain magic in their wake, like diamonds in our memory. I couldn't imagine a more perfect way to usher in the twilight of my visit home.

We hastened inside to alert the family, for surely they'd want to witness this, and found them in the kitchen -- my mom and sister, my brother and his wife, their two young sons and my dad's two wonderful aunts. Gathering at the window, my older nephew, who's all of four, shoved his arms out to me to boost him up. I was a logical choice for him at the moment because I was there and he wanted to see. It took me aback, his coming to an uncle who's little more than a stranger; I didn't even know how to pick him up. What I knew about kids was that I wasn't supposed to curse in front of them and I wasn't supposed to drop them. So, desperate that I'd not mess it up, I finally braced him on the counter between the window and me. Sighting along my arm, he found the deer, fly-sized specks browsing in the grass.

When I dropped my arm to let him watch on his own, I stopped cold. The kitchen lights behind us cast our reflections on the windowglass. I'd been looking out over that familiar field through a spectral image of myself holding Josh and looking older than I'd ever expected myself to get. It was so surreal a vision that my head swam, a glimpse of a life I was once sure I'd never live to see. There was a time I wasn't supposed to see 30.

A few months before this sunset, I was in the visiting room of "The Farm," Maine's minimum-security correctional facility, with Julie Zimmerman and Claudia Whitman, the co-editors of the <u>Frontiers of Justice</u> series. The bare bones of their "Crime Zone" concept had been conceived and hammered out that very weekend and already they were pitching it to me.

"You haven't heard the best part," Claudia gushed, leaning in. "We want you to do the Conclusion." Not a problem, I thought -- I hardly needed convincing!

"And if you're all right with it," Julie added, "we want you to share your story too."

"Okay," I nodded, already seeing aerial photographs of Dresden and Berlin after the war, square miles of roofless building-shells and shattered walls like islands in the rubble. Strange as it may seem, for 12 years now, whenever I think of that December, these are the very images that always leap unbeckoned before my mind's eye: destruction so total it would take years to clear away the wreckage and build anew.

That night, staring at the ceiling after the glow of their encouragement had faded, I questioned their choice of me. While Julie and Claudia contend that I've done well for myself through my years in prison, I insist I've been playing with a stacked deck. I haven't had to face a lot of the challenges so many of my contemporaries have had to overcome -- broken homes and shattered childhoods, exploitation, abject poverty. What little I've managed to achieve pales before the scope of their accomplishments. Few of us inside these places are polished and none are perfected. We are, to a one, works in progress, and when I reflect on those with whom I've shared these journeys, I'm humbled by how far they've come and awed by where many are going. Given the head-starts I was afforded, I sometimes feel like a pretender in their ranks. I am honored to call many of them my friends, the same folks large segments of our society would just as soon forget or prefer to see linger on in perpetual misery.

I finally mentioned my reservations to Julie and told her how I was concerned I might not be representative of many of my fellow inmates. Having come from a stable homelife and a loving, supportive family, I began this odyssey with a good foundation already in place.

"I'm in prison because I was an idiot," I told her. "I'm in here because I threw it all away."

"That's the point, isn't it?" she said, or words to that effect. She reminded me that the faces in our prison system don't belong to other people's children. The more irretrievable predators aside, the chasm between the free and the jailed is, in fact, a thin gray line. Generally speaking, it's often choices, influence and circumstance that separate the innocent from the guilty. Cellblocks are bursting with co-workers, next door neighbors and "other people's children."

I myself was a child raised to believe in family, in work and in God. We were a blue collar family and had blue collar dreams. My parents have been together since high school. My dad's been a firefighter for 34 years and my mom a legislative employee since the mid-1970's. I owe them everything. My mom instilled in me an inquisitive nature, and sowed the seeds for my reliance on faith. My dad gave me an almost pathological work ethic and a belief that integrity for integrity's own sake was essential if I was ever to be a man. I learned to see and appreciate what was around me and I can offer no better an example than the Maine woods. While I will never be the outdoorsman my father and brother are, I now know I was born to such vistas. There were times growing up, alone in the woods, when I truly tasted the spirituality of which my father so often spoke, an inner balance one can only achieve amongst those trees. The forest is a place where man is a guest who's left feeling he very much belongs.

By the time I hit my teenaged years, I was finding fewer places where I felt as at ease. Basically, I was a weird kid and a social retard. I discovered a safety zone within myself early on, finding it easier to live in my books and thoughts than to try and fit in. The older I became and the farther removed from reality, the more this became a defense mechanism; my resentment for the status quo deepened. I was convinced that anyone who went out of their way to fit into any crowd was selling out. I did have some close friends back then, but mostly I felt apart. I became an outsider because it was the path of least resistance; high school dynamics being what they are, most of my fellow students were more than content to keep me at arm's length. The more I was made to feel marginalized by them, the more earnestly I pushed back.

While it would still be a couple of years before they began swimming together, my easy contempt had already found a natural ally in the bottle. In reality, I was drinking alcoholically coming out of the gate. All the classic early symptoms were in place -- my black-outs, how I'd gulp my drinks and my penchant for drinking alone. For a long time, I didn't consider these alcoholic because I felt they were reflective of how I learned to drink in the first place. I was the maintenance boy at a local bowling alley with responsibilities that included cleaning up the place at night. It's basic math: 16 year old boy + untended beer taps = obvious results. Within weeks, I was tapping pitchers of the stuff and leaving them stationed along my cleaning route. There were very few nights I wasn't going home with a respectable buzz on.

Throughout high school, I was convinced my path was set in stone, determined by two disparate influences: my military fascination and my desire, my need, to put Augusta, Maine as far in my rear-view mirror as I could get it. I joined the Army and reported to Ft. Sill, Oklahoma just three weeks after barely graduating high school. On the first morning of basic training, I was thrown from my upper bunk, mattress and all, by a screaming drill sergeant. It was my 18th birthday.

Autumn found me in Germany, beginning what I was certain was my emancipation from all I'd left behind. I was a soldier far from home, a "real man" now, who knew next to nothing about life, though no one could tell me that. In the military, overseas duties were notorious for their debauchery and, burgeoning alcoholic that I was, I dove headlong into it. Back then, many Army units had a laissez faire approach to alcohol abuse. So long as a soldier wasn't undeniably in trouble, which is to say so long as he could stand up and function on duty, a blind eye was generally turned. Alcoholism and military service can and do coexist for protracted periods of time. And it didn't help matters for me that I felt encouraged to pull out all the stops.

Introverted as I was, I had spent the years before trying to remain removed from others, more comfortable in the security of my solitude, never really evolving beyond that. Now, I busily tried to reinvent myself, very much a conscious effort on my part, taking my cues from those who accepted and mirrored my excesses. I built myself with all the skill of an erector set on mescaline. Through with feeling inferior or weak, I strove to be crazier than those around me and found, when I was, I earned a certain respect. If those around me were taking things to the limit, I was the guy anxious to get a step beyond. I was a kid who'd feel a palpable stirring in his chest when I'd see the flag flying over Rivers Barracks upon our return from maneuvers. I was also a kid who, bottle in hand, would hit the brothels, then the nightclubs, staggering back into the barracks in the wee hours and dropping acid rather than going to sleep.

Germany was a vortex of hard work and bacchanal excesses. Half the time, I never even made it back to my room. I'd wake up where I passed out, run four miles, and go about being a soldier. While I smoked pot infrequently in high school, in Germany I discovered drugs. There was no pivotal moment for me, but a quick progression and precipitous decline. If there was a substance to be had, chances are I tried it; if I liked it, chances are I did it a lot. Until the day everything came crashing down around my ears, I was convinced that partying in half measure was cowardly and that those who drank just to be social should stick to badminton.

It was beginning to cost me. The lunacies with which I seasoned my life were taking over. By the time I left Germany, it was out of control and I couldn't stay out of trouble. When I landed in North Carolina, at Ft. Bragg, I could no longer predict what would happen. I couldn't slow down whenever my job demanded it, as I'd been able to only a short time before.

Ft. Bragg took being a soldier more seriously than my last unit and had far less tolerance for substance use. Within a year, I was busted over a drunk and disorderly incident and unceremoniously placed in an outpatient treatment program. By now I knew I was an alcoholic, but was far enough gone that I found it difficult to care. I would show up dutifully for every session, stoned, and strive to tell the counselor everything she wanted to hear with all the sincerity I'd practiced in the mirror that morning. Throughout my time in that program, from which I was graduated as a success short months later, I couldn't get past the idea of how gray and lifeless sobriety seemed to be. I couldn't imagine getting sober, much less wanting to live that way. There could be no joy when the only joy I knew was enmeshed in a "good drunk." I didn't want to stop using; I wanted to stop hurting.

One day, I was talking about life with a poetry-loving, part-time prostitute with whom I'd spent weeks drinking in one of the raunchiest bars in Fayetteville. Sitting at her vanity and rolling a joint, she was telling me her dreams. I sat cross-legged on the floor behind her, bottle of mescal in my lap, stoned cross-eyed on green-bud and pills.

162

"Shoot, I'll never live to see thirty," I told her.

She glanced back at me and cocked her eyebrow, certain I was goofing around.

"You're 21 years old," she accused. "You're too young to be talking that foolishness."

I dumped back a healthy blast of tequila, rinsed my mouth with it and gulped it down.

"Watch me," I said.

I'd been making such declarations for a while by this point, not caring who believed me and who didn't. I knew I was serious. It was logical; giving myself over to it was better than going through life a failure. If I didn't care about living, I shouldn't care about dying, and in that I found liberation. I thus relieved myself of my life's most savage turmoil -- the unending cycle of failing to quit.

Increasingly dissociated with life and identity, I ended my enlistment with little more than my own disillusionment. I stumbled out into the civilian world on inertia. After staying on in North Carolina to await the birth of a good friend's daughter, I did the one thing I thought so unlikely only a short time before: I returned to Augusta. My family was there and it was the only place left where I felt any connection.

After working briefly in construction, only to see my whole crew laid off, I landed a job as a bartender at a Polynesian restaurant. For a self-styled social deviate, it was a sweet gig. Having the keys to a liquor storeroom was the equivalent of a license to steal. And I did. Daily. Within a month, I was bringing a bottle home every night, drinking half to go to sleep on and half to wake up to. The cold beer I was taking into my morning showers to help relieve my hangovers was soon replaced with iced vodka.

I muddled through the summer and into the fall spiraling out of control, though I refused to admit this. I believed I was in active revolt against many of the values with which I was raised, finding them too restrictive and striking increasingly hollow chords in me. The "us versus them" mindset which I'd always had swimming about beneath the surface was becoming pathological. In the middle of that autumn, I finally managed to drink myself out of a job. Fine, I thought, as I was given my walking papers at the end of my shift. I looted the storeroom one last time, grabbing everything I could carry, and marched off into the night. I made it slightly more than 24 hours before I was found drunk on the street by the police, brought to the hospital and had my stomach pumped.

I was taking on roommates by this time, folks who were crashing on whatever floorspace was available, and I was loving it. The apartment had become a perpetual party and I was in my glory. I had already started stealing by this time because my (and then our) expenses outstripped our money. I was getting off on the adrenaline rush that envelopes making a score; so long as I thought no one was getting hurt, it seemed harmless enough.

Being a thief didn't mean I was incapable of getting a job. Keeping one was a different matter. Though it was the end of the season, I got work blacktopping with another construction outfit. I would last less than three weeks, right up till the morning I rolled over, saw more attraction in the lady asleep next to me than the snow that had fallen through the night, rolled over and said, "fuck it." I was sure we were supporting ourselves well enough with all we were stealing and selling. Being divorced from society entitled us to take whatever we could grab and I reckoned we were forging a way of life, one painted by what we believed were our values. There are so few alternative lifestyles when one is white and heterosexual.

It lasted the barest speck of time.

By the end of November, we were out of money, under notice of eviction and I was at complete odds with reality. Still convinced our lifestyle was anything but irresponsible and illusory, we just knew that all we needed was a few good scores and a couple decent breaks and everything would fall into place.

On the night of December 1, 1987, one of my roommates and I set out to commit a robbery, armed with my handgun. We drove around a long time before we finally found the place, smoking dope while I drank. The convenience store we pulled into was selected because it met our two criteria: it was isolated enough to allow us to get away cleanly and it was staffed by a man. Neither Gary nor myself could rob a woman or a senior citizen. We had our standards, after all.

And we robbed the place. Through the years following that night, those close to me have asked if I'd known the clerk would be killed. I give them the only answer I can: I don't know. I didn't take the possibility seriously until the instant he was shot. It happened just that abruptly.

I have few clear memories of the hours that followed, partly from shock and partly because drunk as I'd been wasn't drunk enough. I immediately scored a bottle of cheap whisky and set about drinking myself insensible. Gary and his girlfriend promptly fled the state; I took to wandering the nighttime streets of Augusta on the pretense of ditching the murder weapon, though mostly what I was doing was trying to think my way through it all. There was no doing that. I remember sitting on a guardrail for a fair length of time, trying to sort it out and all of it rioting in my head. I'd crossed a line from which there was no return. We had killed someone -- the very sound of the words felt unreal, though I muttered them a hundred times before the sun came up. All my life, through one scrape after another, I'd been able to worm or weasel my way out, but there was no getting free this time.

A short time later, just before dawn, I was finally hurrying for the river to ditch the gun when I was detained by the Augusta Police for being publicly intoxicated. The lieutenant on duty that night was a family friend and it was unfortunately he who found the pistol when he patted me down.

I have no memory of my arrest; the whisky I'd been dumping into me since the killing pushed me predictably into a black-out. The next "memory snippets" I have are of slowly sobering up, desperately ill and with all the ugly realizations. I was in "the Bricks" of the old Kennebec County Jail. The cell was an observation unit, a drunk tank, that stank of vomit and urine. My clothes had been confiscated for evidence and I had to borrow a child molester's shoes just to have something on my feet when I went for my arraignment that afternoon.

I had never seen more anguish or betrayal in my parents' eyes than I did that morning when they came to the jail. The instant grabbed hold of my every raw nerve and wrenched me to my knees. These are the faces I still see whenever I get to feeling cheaply about my life, reminding me of depths to which I am no longer willing to plunge. I was determined then and there to never put them through such pain again... and yet I was then preparing to up the ante. One of the things that has always struck me as ridiculous whenever I hear the rhetoric of how the death penalty or other such increasingly-harsh punishments are deterrents to crime is that it assumes the offender is even thinking in such terms when his crime occurs. I was sitting in that ghastly little cell with nothing to do but think and panic before "prison" ever entered my mind. For someone who was consciously intending to drink himself to death, suicide wasn't too far a leap.

I was locked in that cell for 23 hours a day in the beginning. During my one hour out for recreation, (meaning I could pace the 50-foot length of the Bricks rather than the 8 of my cage), I snapped a metal plate from the radiator and spent what moments I knew I wasn't being watched honing its jagged edge. Testing my handiwork against my forearm, I drew blood. At 11:00 pm every evening the lights of the jail were dimmed, (they are never turned off), and it was my intention to wait until midnight, after which time the guards in Intake would lose interest in me, and to cut my throat. By the time they noticed, it would have been too late.

That very evening, I got the first mail of my incarceration, a Bible sent by a cousin. Having already read the disclaimer tag on my mattress several times and finding its plot lacking, I spent a good deal of that evening in the Bible, marking time until the lights were dimmed and I could go about my business. I never did get around to cutting my throat despite my most serious intentions. Sometime after midnight, I instead found myself on my knees, praying more earnestly than I ever had in my life. I surrendered. I told God I could no longer live my life, it was over, and if He had plans for me, then I needed Him to bring them on. In that night, in the epicenter of the ugliest period of my life, I felt a peace wash over me like warm water. The peace and new direction were real and have lasted through this very day.

I would spend seven months in jail awaiting trial. During this time, Gary was arrested in Florida and extradited back. I have heard many times how helpless and ignored crime victims feel after the legal process takes over. Ironically, it was little different for me. Mostly the accused do little more than wait it out, languishing in pre-trial detention while the lawyers, prosecutors and investigators hash things out. I spent my time in KCJ trying to hold on and trying desperately to get a toe hold in my new sobriety and faith. I watched the months drag by.

In June of the following year, I pled guilty to being an accessory to the murder and was packed off to begin my life's next season at the Maine State

Prison. Partly my decision was rooted in the convictions with which I'd been raised, to take responsibility for actions, and partly because my lawyer had finally convinced me that those who take their cases to trial almost always serve longer sentences. Gary took his case to trial six months later. They gave him 60 years.

Walking into MSP's notorious East Wing for the first time was like shuffling through a dream, so numbed was I by the experience and shattered by its finality. I had expected prison to be as I'd seen prison in so many movies, with me walking a gauntlet of screaming, taunting convicts. There was little more than long, hard stares and the sounds of morning, the scuffs, coughs and flushing toilets that mark the new day. It would be the first of hundreds of lessons through the weeks that followed that convinced me Hollywood's never gotten it right.

I spent that first evening sitting in a bare cell with the lights off, staring at the walls and listening to the night. The 15½ calendar years in front of me were too unreal to consider, try as I might, and still they crushed me down. I awoke the next morning to the clamor of a cellblock shouting itself awake with crashing steel. It was my 23rd birthday.

The concept of the Crime Zone is rooted in the idea that we, as individuals, have key areas of our lives (self, socialization, spirituality, vocation...) that, when viewed holistically, are inter-reliant. Deficiencies in any one of these categories can adversely affect otherwise stable areas, dragging them into deviance. For example, few could deny that poor, inappropriate or violent social skills will absolutely affect one's sense of self, one's spirituality and vocational potential. My own deficiencies, which included my alcoholism and unhealthy self-image, played key roles in savaging the other quarters of my life, pulling them, pulling me, very much into the Crime Zone, into destructive behaviors.

Conversely, healthy gains in any one of these same areas can have positive and habilitative influences on troubled or crippled areas. Certainly we have all seen the recovering alcoholic or addict's social skills and spirituality blossom after sobriety has been maintained, just as many of us have seen the high school drop-out get her GED, graduate college and change the course of her life. This same dynamic is played out every day in our country's corrections systems, usually in the face of hostility and with inadequate and ever-diminishing support.

Insofar as personal growth, habilitation and reform are concerned, what has been made repeatedly plain throughout the course of the Frontiers of Justice series is that no one solution is universal. Programs and approaches which work well for one segment of our prison populations may have only marginal or no appreciable value for others. With personal demons being at their most malignant when left to fester unaddressed, the universal key to any progress, applicable across the spectrum, seems to be the empowerment of the individual concerned. The prison environment lends itself readily to hopeless-ness, the very thing that makes such a transition most difficult, but when an

166

individual holds a very real stake in his or her progress, in building a healthy life and direction, success rates soar dramatically. Of course, this also implies that these individuals are allowed the tools for such positive growth and direction, something that is becoming increasingly rare in this era's reliance on brick and mortar solutions. It is exhilarating to see that a great number of America's inmates, including several who've been featured in the three volumes of this series, have achieved remarkable progress with grossly inadequate support; surely these achievements are testimonies to human resilience and the innate drive for positive growth. Sadly, in the same breath we must also wonder what those numbers might have been or could be were more adequate support mechanisms in place. I wonder how many we throw away.

Systems of support are essential if any of us, free or incarcerated, hope to rise above adversity. It is in this regard especially that I have been richly blessed and, in fact, have been more fortunate than too many of my brother and sister inmates. My family never wavered a second in supporting me. They began this journey with me horrified, betrayed and grievously hurt, and still they refused to give up on me -- or let me give up on myself. Much of the strength it took to travel what miles I have was given me by them. I doubt I could have been as dogged in my refusal to give up had it not been for my family.

The support and encouragement I've received has not been exclusive to them. Especially through the critical first years of my incarceration, I found myself owing a great debt to MSP's Protestant Chaplain, Rev. Matt Kantrowitz. Bewildered and numbed, I was on spiritually shaky ground, in need of both fellowship and guidance. Matt took a personal interest when it would have been easy to fall away from the fellowship that was so essential to the growth I was pursuing. His pastoral guidance and friendship helped me cement my relationship with Jesus Christ and my reliance on faith. The positive growth and directions I've been pursuing since my incarceration are all rooted in my spirituality. Matt would prove to be the first of many who provided an unbroken chain of support that has helped keep me moving from where I've been to where I hope to go.

In terms of the Crime Zone model, the positive and healthy aspects of my spirituality and familial relationship helped pull the more resistant and troublesome areas of my life into their positive direction, the inverse of what I had been experiencing throughout much of my life and all of my decline. I have seen this same dynamic at work in the lives of so many of the men with whom I've done time and with those I've become familiar with as a result of this series. They, we, reached a watershed in our lives when we found that spark of empowerment upon which we've built. The support structures and opportunities were what we've relied upon once that turning point was reached.

I should also point out that in describing where we've been, none of us have intended to try and use our biographies to excuse or even temper our crimes. We do not blame our pasts but accept responsibility for them. We insist, however, that to understand who we are, and even where we're going, one must understand where we've been. I myself find it difficult to ask for forgiveness; I neither expect it nor feel I've earned it. I've never gotten over my participation in the murder that night. I only know that the one thing in my life I wish I could change, I cannot. I live every day knowing my inability to excise the pain I've inflicted with my life is something that will follow me the rest of my days.

I will be the first to admit that I've truckloads of improvement left to accomplish, but what successes and growth I've earned were realized only after I was allowed, and allowed myself, to achieve a splinter of hope. It began with a choice between life and death and diving, finally and voraciously, into what I'd been certain was the more difficult of the two. I decided to live.

It was the face of a 34-year old man staring back at me from the windowglass, young nephew in his arms, still unsure how he'd managed to come to be standing in front of that window. It was the face of a man with 12 years in prison behind him, with three more to go and a glimpse of a life both immediately familiar and foreign.

"Deer," Josh said, pointing out through our reflections to the back field. He blurted it out with his whole upper body in the way small children do, swelling his ribs against my arms when he said it. I was just about his age when my dad pointed out my first deer to me. Josh's head was at my cheek and I pushed my face into hair still smelling of shampoo. A part of me sobbed.

Scott Antworth *is a two-time PEN Prisoner Writing Award winner (1998 & 1999). He graduated with distinction from the University of Maine at Augusta while a guest of the Maine State Prison. He remains incarcerated at a minimum-security work farm. After making his debut in Biddle Publishing's collection, <u>Trapped Under Ice</u>, he has since been included in their anthology, <u>Frontiers of Justice, Volume 2</u>. His fiction is regularly featured in <u>Flying Horse</u>, has appeared in <u>Doing Time: 25 Years of PEN Prison Writing</u> and is forthcoming in both <u>Best New American Voices 2000</u> and <u>Out of Line</u>. He is currently at work on his first novel. Scott is also an artist and craftsman.*

Photo credit: Brian Vandenbrink Photo © 2000

EPILOGUE

When a crime is committed and the early media reports come in, the editors of this volume, like you, feel outrage, a kneejerk response that the perpetrator should experience the same pain and fear as the victim, or worse. Later, we watch him in the courtroom, (looking "unrepentant" according to the press), and wish he would suddenly understand the gravity and repercussions of his actions. We want him overcome with guilt, crying for the victim, not over the loss of his own freedom.

But behind the offender's courtroom face is a person. The guy on your TV screen may well be unrepentant; most likely he is angry, delusional, terrified or in shock, maybe trying desperately to follow his attorney's instruction and not show any emotion to those damn TV cameras. Some will remain defiant or delusional. But many would do anything to undo the harm they did.

Given the pain and losses of the victim and victim's family, it is easy to believe the offender to be monster, enemy, devil, thereby justifying any punishment, any humiliation. Whatever our prison system can dish out, he deserves it! Capital punishment is an example. There is no question that murder is wrong, yet 38 states emulate the murderer. They send the message to every American that killing does solve our worst problems. We can even convince ourselves that juvenile offenders as young as 11 or 12 should be tried as adults and put away for life. A vicious crime does not magically turn an adolescent into an adult; he remains a deeply troubled child. What was happening to that same child a few years earlier when no one intervened?

This book's editors and contributors are not naive enough to think that our efforts will change Americans' views about crime and corrections, but we do have two dreams. The first is that we will see the end of capital punishment in the United States in our lifetimes, (and that another "tough on crime" frenzy won't usher it back a few years later). It is with this vision that we dedicate Frontiers of Justice, Volume 3: The Crime Zone to A.J. Bannister, Clifford Boggess, Brian Baldwin and Billy Hughes. These four men were all a part of the Frontiers of Justice project and message. They were executed (respectively) by the states of Missouri, Texas, Alabama and Texas. They were put to death as murderers, nothing more, but we knew them as men with artistic talent, generous natures, humor and vast capacities for friendship.

171

Our second dream is that the readers of the <u>Frontiers of Justice</u> series will come to see criminals as more than just the crimes they committed. They are people who have caused great harm and are responsible for their actions, but they are also human beings in need of help. This country must care about its young children and protect them. We must do a better job of intervening on behalf of troubled teens and juvenile offenders. We must recognize that turning 18 or being classified as an adult does not disqualify an offender from the potential for growth and change. Not only is this "the right thing to do," it is a safer, more effective, less expensive solution for our society.

We are one country. We can work to develop a system that protects society and supports victims, while at the same time doing more than warehousing offenders in environments that foster mental illness, rage, racism, dehumanization, brutalization and death.

May this volume advance that dream.

Claudia Whitman
Julie Zimmerman

Claudia Whitman is a collage artist who divides her time between Colorado and Maine. She has toured parts of the country with a collaboration of her art and death row inmate Gene Hathorn's poetry to promote dialogue about capital punishment. She co-edited <u>Frontiers of Justice, Volumes 1 & 2</u>, and works with Equal Justice, U.S.A. as a member of the editorial board on their upcoming book, <u>Saga of Shame</u>. Claudia is a penpal and visitor to prisoners across the country, and takes on special projects to support these friends. She is working to establish The Juno Center, a non-profit organization to advance the message of humane criminal justice. She and her husband, Laird, publish the online magazine, <u>CellDoor</u>.

Julie Zimmerman graduated from Swarthmore College in 1968 and had a career as a Physical Therapist specializing in the treatment of developmentally disabled children. At age 37, Julie became physically disabled; she authored a book for school therapists, still widely used, as a farewell to her profession. She was one of the founders of an AIDS education/support group in her community. Julie has authored five books, edited four books and helped nine incarcerated authors get their books into print. In 1998, she was awarded Maine's Intellectual Freedom Award for her work in criminal justice. Julie lives on the coast of Maine with her husband and a menagerie of dogs, cats and chickens.

INDEX

substance abuse 26-27, 48-53, 94, 147-149, 154-155, 162-164
substance abuse programs/counseling 18, 28, 30, 76-77, 95-96, 98-100
Substance Abuse Training Program 76-77
suicide 15, 17, 165
supermax prisons 7

Texas judicial system 125-126
theft (see robbery)
tough on crime 77, 111
Tucker, Willie Christopher 71-81
"two strikes" law (see tough on crime)

university programs (see college programs)

Vermont State Prison 28, 30
victim restitution 111
violence in prison 62
vocational training 18, 56-57, 150

Wenatchee, WA case 133-134
Willard Treatment Center 99
women in prison 40-46
writing 18

Youth Assistant Programs 100
youth intervention programs 100-101

The authors of <u>Frontiers of Justice, Volume 3: The Crime Zone</u>
welcome your comments and correspondence.
You can write them
c/o Biddle Publishing Company
PMB 103, PO Box 1305
Brunswick ME 04011.

BIDDLE PUBLISHING CO. CRIMINAL JUSTICE TITLES

Frontiers of Justice, Vol. 1: The Death Penalty

This powerful anthology represents inmates, their families and their victims' families as well as professionals in the areas of law, criminal justice, government, religion, journalism and advocacy. These authors, both the incarcerated and the free, deplore the use of legalized killing to solve America's criminal justice problems. Introduction by Mario Cuomo. *"...a phenomenal job in bringing together eloquent anti-death penalty views.... As long as we command the state to perform executions for us, we perpetuate the act of murder... If ever we wish to change, this book will be part of the reason why."* Edward Asner

Frontiers of Justice, Vol. 2: Coddling or Common Sense?

The authors of this anthology range from volunteers to professionals in law, law enforcement and corrections, from crime victims to offenders. They represent humane, successful programs in both prisons and the community for both juveniles and adults. Turning away from revenge-based criminal justice is not only less costly and more effective in preventing crime and lowering recidivism. It also preserves the human dignity of us all. Introduction by Ramsey Clark. *"This is a stunning collection of stories of 'at risk' people who are making it back to something akin to stability, normalcy, productivity -- because someone cared enough to try to help. It's not a Pollyanna story; it's a book, chapter and verse account of what works and what doesn't, and why Americans should shed their skepticism and pitch in."* Mike Wallace

Other Biddle Publishing/Audenreed Press Titles:

Caged Freedom (Osei Cotton)	Dead End (Gary Goldhammer)
Going to Prison? (Jimmy Tayoun)	Iowa on the Inside (Vincent Johnson)
Practical Reformation (Calbraith MacLeod)	Self Land (Gene Hathorn)
Shall Suffer Death (A.J. Bannister)	The Warden Wore Pink (Tekla Miller)

Trapped Under Ice: A Death Row Anthology (Ed. Julie Zimmerman)

Prisoners' Guerrilla Handbook to Correspondence Programs (Jon Marc Taylor)

These titles can be ordered by calling the publisher at 1-888-315-0582, special ordering at any bookstore or on the web at biddle-audenreed.com or at Barnes&Noble.com.